REVOLUTIONARY VIOLENCE

Urban Terrorism: Theory, Practice and Response, Leo Cooper, 1975

The Destruction of Loyalty, Foreign Affairs Research Institute, Whitehall, London, 1976

REVOLUTIONARY VIOLENCE

The Theories

ANTHONY BURTON

C_R

Crane, Russak & Company, Inc.
NEW YORK

Published in the United States by

Crane, Russak & Company, Inc.
347 Madison Avenue
New York, New York 10017

First published in Great Britain by
Leo Cooper Ltd
196 Shaftesbury Avenue
London WC2H 8JL England

ISBN 0-8448-1262-5

LC 77-83808

Printed in Great Britain

JC
491
B85
1978

76755

CONTENTS

ILLUSTRATIONS

The author and publishers are grateful to the *Radio Times*
Hulton Picture Library for permission to reproduce
illustrations nos. 1, 2, 3 and 4, and to the Associated Press
for permission to reproduce illustrations nos. 5, 6, 7, 8
and 9.

PREFACE

This book is the first of three on the subject of revolutionary violence; further volumes will cover case studies and counter-revolutionary theory and practice.

Acknowledgement is due to Jonathan Cape Ltd and the Seven Pillars Trust for the extracts from *Seven Pillars of Wisdom* by T. E. Lawrence and to MacGibbon & Kee/ Granada Publishing Ltd for *The Wretched of the Earth* by Frantz Fanon.

ANTHONY BURTON

August, 1977

ix

CHAPTER 1

Revolution and Violence: The State of the Art

'Now insurrection is an art quite as much as war or any other and subject to certain rules of proceeding'.

ENGELS

Among the greatest enemies of the next revolution are the academic theorists who write about the last one. This is particularly the case where the authors involved are sympathetic to the persons or the ideologies of the revolutionaries. Lessons which are too neat and principles which are too vague are generalized from the exploits of some revolutionary hero, while failures are explained away. 'Models' of revolution are produced. Thus we have a Leninist, a Maoist and a Guevarist model whose contemporary Western adherents indulge in abstruse and often irrelevant arguments.[1]

Academic theorists tend to underestimate the primitive forces of tribalism and racialism from which they imagine themselves to have been freed. Their preference for sweepingly general economic and 'class' explanations rather than the more specific and primitive is reinforced by other factors: Marxism, with its emphasis on bourgeois/proletarian instead of national characteristics appeals to the modern University élite and international academic contact provides an alternative community to that of the nation. The large proportion of those of émigré origin in intellectual circles (especially in sociology) is also naturally sympathetic to such an approach.

1

The fostering of the myth of the revolutionary guerrilla has been one of the means whereby the older generation has betrayed the younger. Régis Debray, the French philosopher and interpreter of the Cuban Revolution, has been widely read. His remarks, from the point of view of actually fighting a guerrilla war, are unhelpful. The 'guerrillas of Teoponte', students who went into the hostility of total jungle with little more than sandwiches, were victims of this kind of romantic stupidity.[2] Che Guevara's failure and death in Bolivia were the result of his coming to believe in the myth which had grown up around him, and which Debray had helped to create. Not one Bolivian peasant joined Che's band; as one of his followers sadly remarked, 'They never understood us'. Talk of a 'continental revolution' in South America underestimated the ethnic, cultural, linguistic and economic differences involved. Middle-class would-be revolutionaries have nowhere communicated effectively with the people they hoped to liberate. In Uruguay the TUPAMAROS' rural campaign was a disaster, despite the fact that their leader, Sendic, had originally been an organizer of sugarcane workers. In their rural operations the student-based TUPAMAROS failed to bridge the cultural gap between them and the population.

Revolutionary expectations in Western democracies have also been disappointed because those who have held them have been at the same time contemptuous of national traditions. Many Communists and Trotskyists have been of different ethnic origin from the majority of their target populations. 'Foreigners' rarely carry political credibility. In Britain the revolutionary Left has been heavily weighted with the type of Englishmen who, as Georges Sorel perceptively observed, believe that 'by humiliating their country they will arouse more sympathy towards themselves'.[3] Such a belief has not been borne out by history.

A further characteristic of the academic commentator, which is exaggerated by the prejudices and selective inattention of his students, is a gross underestimation of the inert weight of the *status quo*. To this is added an ignorant contempt for the intelligence of the Police and Army. Young revolutionaries too frequently believe that those who have not been accorded their vision of a 'brave new world' are intellectually bankrupt. Characterizing police as 'pigs' and opponents as 'Fascists' may be at times a rational political tactic but it precludes any appeal to *their* grievances. It dehumanizes 'the enemy' to the point where he is seen as a cardboard caricature, inflexibly incapable of imagination and initiative. In Britain fringe-group Trotskyists have shown this kind of Pavlovian reaction to Army counter-insurgency experts, refusing to see them in human terms but only as 'class enemies'.

If one goes to the experiences and early publications of successful revolutionaries, then the picture changes drastically. Speeches, writings and tactics contemporary to the actual fighting of the revolutionary war (not later rationalizations) show two outstanding common characteristics. They involve appeals to collective pride and individual greed, and they are voiced in *national* terms by men who are *of the people*. Above all, the leaders of revolutionary wars have understood, not abstract theories culled from books, but the populations they sought to influence. As Mao Tse-tung remarked, 'It is evident that to read too many books is harmful . . . the question is whether your direction is right or not'.[4] Lenin, according to Radek, 'smelt of Russia'. In China, Mao took care to be seen as the leading fighter for Chinese dignity against the Japanese. Ho Chi Minh placed himself at the head of 'united front' organizations seeking, not proletarian revolution, but self-determination and independence. Traditional, not Marxist–Leninist, virtues[5] were regarded by Ho as paramount. Kim Il Sung found appeals to racial, cultural and national sentiment in Korea much more effective than any exhortations to be good Marxist–Leninists.[6]

In this situation it is not surprising that the activists of the West have had no more success in peddling their revolutionary wares than did the idealistic young Populists of nineteenth-century Russia. The current passion for sociology has hindered revolutionary politics since it has led to the adoption of symbolic rather than actual involvement; striking ideologically proper attitudes has been preferred to hard work.

In the classic cases of Russia, China and Vietnam violence was accepted and used against foreign invaders and their lackeys in the name of national pride. Where violence could not be seen in these terms, as in Malaya after the Second World War, it was less effective. Identification with foreign influence, from Cuba or the USSR for example, has been damaging to revolutionary movements, especially in South America. Those groups which could at least claim to be national in personnel and aims (however much clandestine support from abroad they in fact received) have come closest to success (e.g. in Uruguay and Venezuela). In the West the Provisional IRA and Basque ETA, which take their inspiration from nationalism, even if their language is frequently Marxist, have achieved and maintained a degree of support for a campaign of violence in excess of that mounted by any 'revolutionary' movement. Nationalism (and lesser tribalisms such as religion) has continued to be the main inspiration of the wars and insurrections of our time.[7]

Revolution and Violence—political or cathartic?
Diversity in the motives of those involved cannot obscure a basic distinction between revolutionary violence as a political tactic and contrasting sociological, psychological or, occasionally, mystical explanations.

Revolution may be seen as an essentially political act— the changing within a State not just of a Government but of its accompanying social order. It is possible, of course, to speak of *revolutionary changes* in units either smaller or larger than the State. Thus part of a federation, or an institution within the State, such as a University, might be

4

described as having 'undergone a revolution'. In terms of conventional political categorization such changes may be in a Right as well as a Left Wing direction. Alternatively revolution can be seen as lying altogether outside the categories of nation and state. In this case the revolutionary regards the basis of relationships between groups as being *class* not *nation*. An opposite example of this same tendency is the replacement of *nation* by *race*, as, for example, in Nazi ideas of Aryan identity as determining élite status.

The political category of revolution may be further subdivided into *separatist* and *internal*. In the former case the overriding aim is the transfer of decision-making from an external to a local body; this will mean the ejection of troops and officials seen as 'foreign'. A programme of social and economic reform will invariably be proposed but this may involve no more than a change of emphasis and personalities. The *separatist* need offer no sophisticated ideological alternative to the Government; it is enough if he can fix blame on it.

If the *status quo* is to be altered more radically, however, and there are no 'foreign oppressors' to create a nationalist revolutionary unity, then the task of the insurgent is much more complex. What is sought is not some conceptually simple 'freedom from domination' but complex and radical changes in social structure, modes of life and ways of thought. Here the *revolutionary* has to work out the dimensions of his alternative society in great detail and even then is likely to succeed only through a simultaneous crisis in the Government. This crisis situation may be brought about by sudden and bewildering changes in the accepted pattern of life, for example by war or rapid inflation.

Leading actors in the political drama will perceive their roles in different ways. They may regard themselves as behaving in conformity with laws whose inevitable operation they have foreseen, so that to act otherwise would be to go against the forces of history. Such an approach gives rise to

5

an assurance of victory and assertions that 'We will bury you,' 'The future is ours, Comrade,' and so on.

In contrast there is the entirely subjective approach in which man is regarded as capable of creating his own future by choosing from among a number of options.

In extreme forms these two views, one fatalistic, the other creative, characterize the struggle within revolutionary movements, often between generations. Debray's book *Revolution in the Revolution*,[8] with its ideas of 'creating the revolution' out of the guerrilla band almost by a romantic act of will, contrasts with the weary pessimism of older Party hacks for whom 'objective conditions' are never quite ripe for revolution.

There is finally the possibility of a 'moral' approach in which only certain principles or norms of action are held to be fixed. By adapting these norms to particular situations, the revolutionary can be creative at the same time—for example by extending the Maoist principle of the countryside surrounding the towns to the whole world, where the poor nations can similarly surround the rich.

An examination of revolutions (defined in this case as being 'socialist' and in the direction of a 'classless' society) by Galtung[9] produced a total of fourteen: the Soviet Union and its *bloc* (nine), plus Cuba, Yugoslavia,Vietnam, North Korea and China. The majority of these were feudal or pre-capitalist countries, all were reactions to foreign domination rather than to capitalism (i.e. nationalist rather than proletarian); World War was invariably involved and the West was too far away to interfere effectively, the only exception to those characteristics being Cuba (the Cuban Revolution became Marxist at a comparatively late stage, the United States was thus taken by surprise). Finally, in all cases the previous régime could be regarded as oppressive.

One must conclude that from the point of view of the revolutionary seeking political change in the nation-state the outlook is not encouraging; the conditions outlined above are unlikely to recur. War is as likely to result in a battle

6

for animal survival as to be an engine of social change. Nationalism is certainly not dead but the forms it takes politically are frequently not even radical, let alone revolutionary. Governments have greater power than ever before to deal with counter-State activity, especially given their control, actual or potential, of the mass-media. Provided Governments are flexible enough to syphon off possible revolutionary energy by allowing social and geographical mobility, they can prevent the formation of frustrated élites from which revolutionary leaders might arise.

It is true that inflation, economic depression and civil violence still offer opportunities to the revolutionary. Such conditions reduce the Government's chances of meeting grievances through sponsoring social change. The Government cannot afford the money to innovate. The centre ground tends to be deserted in favour of extreme solutions or easy panaceas, while the authorities lack the wherewithal to bribe the people back again. Allegedly, it is because economic growth has enabled the American establishment to 'buy' their working class that some have seen marginal elements (students, negroes, Puerto Ricans etc) as constituting the 'revolutionary potential' in that country. However, despite these factors, there seems little evidence that the apathetic multitude are anywhere near insurrection. Even if a crisis point is reached the result is as likely to be a totalitarian Government of the Right as of the Left (as occurred in Uruguay, where the TUPAMAROS guerillas succeeded in replacing a relatively liberal Government, not by Socialism, but by military domination).

In all these cases revolution is conceived by Government and insurgent alike as a political act. Revolutionary violence, therefore, and the reaction to it, must be an expression of political logic. Demonstrations, riots, robberies, guerrilla actions, revolutionary war—throughout the whole process must run the thread of political relevance. Such actions are different in degree, but not in kind, from writing, making speeches, voting or writing to the newspapers. The aim is not to kill or destroy property, but to influence Governments and peoples. Perception is the target, not blood on the streets. The revolutionary who follows these precepts is using violence in the tradition of the great Prussian philosopher of war, Carl Maria von Clausewitz.

People's War was, to Clausewitz, supplementary to the operations of a regular Army, particularly in the defensive role where an aggressor has succeeded in invading his enemy's country. Clausewitz foresaw that as a result of economic and technical change the boundaries of 'war' would move from professional to total involvement. 'A People's War in general,' he said, 'is to be regarded as a consequence of the outburst which the military element in our day has made through its old formal limits.'[10]

Since, to Clausewitz, war is a struggle between States then naturally guerrilla warfare is subordinate and relative to the political objectives involved. Led, trained and stiffened by a few professional soldiers, the guerrilla could operate in a situation of protracted war to harass the enemy and gradually destroy his supply organization. To Clausewitz the best conditions for guerrilla warfare were a people accustomed to poverty operating in tough country. Ideally there should also be a base area from the security of which attacks could be mounted in order to create an impression of 'uneasiness and dread'. A neighbouring country friendly to the insurgent might provide the best of all base areas, since the enemy could not pursue the guerrillas without running the risk of widening the conflict.

Similar considerations apply in the case of revolutionary violence short of war. Such violence, like Clausewitzian war, has 'its own grammar but not its own logic'. The logic is provided by the political aim. Classifications of guerrilla warfare in support of revolutionary objectives are all relative to the importance of the political aim, which is not necessarily served by trying to decide which category applies. Techniques of revolutionary violence are only as good as their political impact.

Revolution in a modern State is a hopeless undertaking if classical models are followed. Suddenly to overturn the social structure of such a State requires a degree of social unrest and access to organizational power which can both be denied by Governments. Neither Lenin nor Mao can create another revolution, still less Guevara. Revolutionary violence and war have not succeeded in South America despite a superficially favourable environment and foreign encouragement. As an offensive technique for overthrowing Governments, guerrilla tactics look anachronistic. However, as a defensive technique for raising the cost of attack to a level unacceptable to a potential invader, they seem more promising. This point was of course made by Clausewitz; the whole people becomes a guerrilla army, offering active harassment and non-co-operation to the invading forces. Paradoxically, tactics perfected to upset the *status quo* may now be used by perceptive Governments as a prop for it!

The fact that the age of revolutionary war appears to be over does not mean that revolutionary violence can no longer be employed. Indeed, the phrase 'revolutionary war' is already taking on a new meaning. Just as in the context of war between States there is now an accepted category of 'limited war', where the aim is to 'affect the enemy's will, not to break it', so there is now developing a kind of 'limited revolutionary violence'.

Instead of attacking the nation-state outright, the new revolutionary selects a specific demand or area of weakness and uses violence to extract concessions at that particular point.

Revolutionary violence is used as a pressure-group tactic. It is linked to other activities to achieve a limited and precise aim. This aim is short-term and attainable.

Targets have been switched, and hence the methodology has also changed. Operations are now almost entirely 'psycho-military'. The aim is to influence, not just national Governments, but decision-making bodies generally. Sometimes these targets may be Government agencies, sometimes international bodies (for example, the United Nations, the European Economic Community or the Organization of Petroleum Exporting Countries) or they may be more nebulous—world opinion, or public opinion within an area, State or group. Perceptions of, for example, Jews, the British or the Chileans will be affected by attacking their property, their institutions and their representatives abroad. While ultimately seeking revolution in a given State or area, the revolutionary is content to proceed by means of a number of intermediate steps which, to others, may appear to have little connection with revolution.

In one sense the targets of this new pressure-group revolutionary activity have narrowed; in another they have widened. Since this type of terrorist has no requirement to tie his activities to any one country he is able to ignore all conventions. The *system* which denies him the autonomy which he seeks is equally his enemy. Thus people and locations apparently totally removed from any connection with his grievance become involved. The revolutionary certainly perceives a connection—economic, propagandistic or cultural—between his target and his grievance, but the victims don't and the police, not sharing the same frame of reference, and unable to predict even if they did, are frequently taken by surprise. So we have a new phenomenon: revolutionary war against all, anywhere, at any time, totally subversive of the international system and international order. Supporting this strategy is a revolutionary sub-culture, with its own counter-system.

Lack of political success in classical revolutionary terms has led to another alternative approach. Instead of trying to find a new political dimension in which to operate, as has international terrorism, there has been a tendency to switch the emphasis away from the political altogether. Violence and participation in revolutionary struggle have been seen as leading to social group cohesion and personal satisfaction.

Here violence is not primarily seen in political terms at all. We may trace this type of attitude historically to rebel figures such as the Brazilian Lampiao or to the Sicilian bandit, Salvatore Guiliano. Anarchist theory, which sees the revolutionary elements in society as being the outcasts and criminals, lies in this tradition. Today, in a situation where the proletariat appears mainly concerned with getting rich as quickly as possible, the revolutionary naturally looks elsewhere for his human material.

There are a number of variants of this cathartic approach to violence: it may be seen as racially or ethnically creative, personally liberating or socially functional.

Groups as different as the Jewish IRGUN and Black Power movements have seen violence as creating a new identity. To the IRGUN ZVEI LEUMI, the use of violence could change the stereotype of the Jew and help to forge a new solidarity and sense of nationhood: 'we fight therefore we are'.

Black Power movements were influenced by the writings of Frantz Fanon. Born and educated in Martinique, Fanon discovered that in Europe French cultural identity could not compensate for a black skin. He studied medicine in Lyons and later became a psychiatrist. Black people, he argued, and indeed the oppressed generally, internalize the social situation: individual stresses are the result of social tensions. In order to change the individual, his relationship to the social/political environment must be dramatically transformed. No amount of introspection or rationalization can overcome the incompleteness of the black man. Not by adopting a European mask, nor by retiring into a cultural ghetto, but only by the assertion of political freedom *now*, can self-fulfilment occur. Therein lay the path to mental health and happiness. Revolutionary violence was good medicine.

Working as a doctor during the Algerian uprising, Fanon saw the results of terrorism in terms of individual horror.

11

He came to believe that racialism was an essential accompaniment to colonialism, justifying and buttressing its hold over black men. Break colonialism and you destroy racialism. Revolution was the way to attack colonialism and set the black man personally as well as politically free. Fanon's at times extravagant prose spread his message, at least to intellectuals, and particularly to black revolutionary movements in the West. Fanon was providing a social myth which would give a frame of reference and an inspiration to those who felt themselves to be oppressed. Violence could forge a new nation of new men who would be able to continue on the path of heroic self-fulfilment after the revolution had been achieved.

In his most influential book, *The Wretched of the Earth*, Fanon sees the outcasts of society, who are beyond charity but not beyond redemption, being 'saved' by participation in revolutionary violence. De-colonization comes after a 'decisive and murderous confrontation of the two protagonists' which turns the colonized 'object' into a man. The deep self-destructive urge is worked out in action:

> Violence alone, violence committed by the people, violence educated and organized by its leaders makes it possible for the masses to understand social truths and gives the key to them . . . at the level of individuals violence is a cleansing force . . . (it) frees the native from his inferiority complex and from his despair and inaction; it makes him fearless and restores his self-respect.[11]

Fanon died in 1961, thirty-six years old. Perhaps the high tide of his influence was in the late 1960s when his book was used both by Black Power militants and by white students. BLACK PANTHER PARTY theorist Eldridge Cleaver wrote of Fanon's *The Wretched of the Earth*:

> What this book does is to legitimize the revolutionary impulse to violence. It teaches colonial subjects that it is

12

perfectly normal for them to rise up and cut off the heads of their slavemasters, that it is a way to achieve their manhood, and that they must oppose the oppressors in order to experience themselves as men.[12]

Some white students, too, felt that they could wrench free from class guilt and purge themselves of 'bourgeois hang-ups' by a violence similar to that advocated by Fanon for Black emancipation.

Vallières' idealogue of the urban guerrilla FRONT FOR THE LIBERATION OF QUEBEC, caught the flavour of this approach with his portrayal of French Canadians as *White Negroes of America*.[13] Yet Fanon's 'revolution as catharsis' does not represent simply a passing phase, it lies deep in revolutionary tradition.

The violent version of anarchism, for example, seems as much designed to meet the individual problems of the terrorist as those of society in general. Since the anarchist does not imagine that his actions will bring any immediate change in society he has historically been prepared to sacrifice himself in order to produce an increment in the process of eroding the social and political order. This element of self-immolation was shown in the late nineteenth and early twentieth centuries by anarchists who, far from seeking to escape from the police, offered themselves to the authorities as examples of revolutionary dedication. Contrasting tactics today such as the anonymous planting of bombs in doorways thus constitute a betrayal of these historical traditions.

Nechayev, the archetype of the nineteenth century anarchist terrorist, while less impressive in action than in the violence of his words, emphasized the individual commitment required: the revolutionary must 'tear himself free from the bonds of the social order and the civilized world'. Sacco and Vanzetti, Italian anarchists executed in the United States in 1927, symbolized the martyrdom of the individual anarchist. Vanzetti's oft-quoted statement exemplifies the traditional anarchist attitude:

13

If it had not been for this case, I might have lived out my life, talking on street corners to scorning men. I might have died, unmarked, unknown, a failure . . . our words, our lives, our pains—nothing! The taking of our lives— lives of a good shoemaker and a poor fish peddler—all. The last moment belongs to us—that agony is our triumph.

Today the writings of Herbert Marcuse, which for a while competed with those of Fanon and the *Thoughts of Chairman Mao* as basic reading for revolutionary students, also suggest the individual benefits to be gained from attempting to overthrow the contemporary political order. Like Fanon, Marcuse re-interprets Freud: man's individual psychological problems must be met by political action. Get rid of the present evil order and man will be re-born without his destructive urges—which are but a reaction to the oppressive forces of Government and authority. In *A Critique of Pure Tolerance*[14] Marcuse advocates what amounts to a totalitarian attitude to the 'fascism' of the Right; in place of 'pure tolerance' he offers selective tolerance. There should be a 'withdrawal of tolerance from regressive movements . . . intolerance even toward thought, opinion and word, and, finally, intolerance in the opposite direction, that is, toward the self-styled conservatives, to the political Right—these anti-democratic notions respond to the actual development of the democratic society which has destroyed the basis of universal tolerance.'[15]

Elsewhere[16] Marcuse argues that there exists in society 'surplus repression' needed to maintain the political domination of the system: remove it, and Utopia is possible. This can also be understood on the personal level, men ought to liberate themselves from the miseries of alienation imposed by industrial society.

In *One Dimensional Man*[17] Marcuse sees liberalism as the most subtle form of manipulation because it fools people into thinking that it is meeting their needs when it is in fact exploiting them.

14

How can all this be changed? Marcuse envisages the social outcast as the cannon fodder of revolution. It is 'the exploited and persecuted of other races and colours, the unemployed and the unemployable' whose 'opposition is an elementary force that violates the rules of the game.'[18] Here is the new proletariat through whose violence both new social order and new man may be born. For Marcuse agrees that the destruction of the existing order will require violence ('counter violence' in his terminology). Violence is creative if it comes from below, from the 'oppressed'. To the student revolutionaries (particularly of the 'sixties) violence had two functions: it was necessary to break the political order—and *that* was necessary for psychological freedom. Political and psychological freedom would both come through revotionary violence.

Some fifty years before Marcuse a different but more influential justification of revolutionary violence had been given by Georges Sorel. *Reflections on Violence*, Sorel's most famous work, appeared in 1906. To Sorel violence is socially functional; if the proletariat is to be politically virile it must be opposed by a confident and aggressive middleclass:

> The more ardently capitalist the middle-class is, the more the proletariat is full of a warlike spirit and confident of its revolutionary strength, the more certain will be the success of the proletarian movement.[19]

Marx expressed the same concept when he wrote: 'So that one class *par excellence* may appear as the class of liberation, another class must conversely be the manifest class of oppression.'[20] Everything might be saved, asserted Sorel, 'if the proletariat, by their use of violence, manage to re-establish the division into classes . . . proletarian violence, carried on as a pure and simple manifestation of the class war, appears to us as a very fine and very heroic thing'.[21]

15

Progress comes from the clash of these class opposites. In order to arouse the masses there must be in addition a *myth* which explains the past and holds out the vision of a brave new world. Passionately believing in the myth, personifying and interpreting it, is the small élite band of professional revolutionaries. The people will accept the inevitability of their misery until roused into realization by the propaganda of the deed. Mussolini seized gratefully on this useful theory while Sorel himself, just before his death in 1922, imagined that his charismatic band of revolutionaries had been made flesh in the persons of the Bolsheviks! Nazis, Mussolini's Fascists, Leninists and Guevarists all share a common belief in the efficacy of the disciplined band of élite professionals to create revolution through action.

Thus motives for revolutionary violence may take a number of forms, ranging from political logic to psychological need. In any one revolutionary movement motives will naturally be mixed; the leaders may have a political programme but those who belong to the lower echelons of the organization may exhibit any or all of the attitudes mentioned above. Such considerations make the response to revolutionary violence a complicated matter involving not only political judgment, but sensitivity to sociological issues and psychological analysis. Clearly the response must be relative to the nature of the violence and take account of the motivation of those involved. Each specific challenge must be met on all these levels. If the revolutionary movement is to be met effectively, it must be on the basis of a careful preceding analysis of the economic and social conditions on which it is seeking to rely. Technological substitutes for intelligent thought will make matters worse: you cannot napalm people into supporting you. Violence within the State and aggressions from outside it which use revolutionary tactics as 'surrogates' for direct attacks cannot be met by the kind of blinkered military response which 'counts wisdom no member of the war'.[22] We must by 'reason and knowledge guide' the formation and execution of policy

—and it is this requirement which justifies this chapter and
those which follow.

NOTES

1　A conference of the American *Students for a Democratic
Society* degenerated into a slanging match: one faction chant-
ing 'Ho, Ho, Ho Chi Minh', while the other bawled 'Mao, Mao,
Mao Tse-tung'
2　Burton, Anthony, *Urban Terrorism*, Leo Cooper, London and
Free Press of New York, 1975, p 78
3　Sorel, Georges, *Reflections on Violence*, trans Hulme, Collier-
Macmillan 1950, p 79
4　*Mao Tse-tung Unrehearsed*, ed. Schram, Pelican, 1974, pp. 118
and 204
5　Diligence, frugality, justice and integrity; see Fenn, Charles,
Ho Chi Minh, Studio Vista, London, 1973, pp 40 and 96
6　Scalopino, Robert and Lee, Chong-sik, *Communism in Korea*,
University of California Press, 1973
7　See Brodie, Bernard, *War and Politics*, Cassell, 1974, p 317
8　MR Press, 1967
9　Galtung, Johan, *A Structural Theory of Revolutions*, Rotter-
dam University Press, 1974
10　Clausewitz, *On War*, ed Maude, Routledge and Kegan Paul,
1949, p 341
11　Fanon, Frantz, *The Wretched of the Earth*, trans Farrington,
Penguin, 1967, p 74
12　Cleaver, Eldridge, *Post-Prison Writings and Speeches*, New
York, 1969, p 20
13　In his autobiography of the same name, published in 1968
14　Marcuse, Herbert, *A Critique of Pure Tolerance*, Beacon Press,
1966
15　Marcuse, op cit, p 110
16　In *Eros and Civilisation: a Philosophical Enquiry into Freud*,
Beacon Press and Vantage Books, 1955
17　Beacon Press, 1964
18　*One Dimensional Man*, p 256
19　Sorel, op cit, p 88–89
20　Karl Marx, *Early Texts*, ed. McLellan, Oxford, 1971, p 126
21　Sorel, op cit, p 98
22　Shakespeare, *Troilus and Cressida*, Act I, Scene iii, in which the
narrowly military approach to war is soundly castigated:

17

They tax our policy, and call it cowardice,
Count wisdom no member of the war,
. . . esteem no act
But that of hand: the still and mental parts
. . . hath not a finger's dignity;
They call this bed-work, mappery, closet war;
So that the ram that batters down the wall,
For the great swing and rudeness of his poise,
They place before his hand that made the engine,
Or those that with the fineness of their souls
By reason guide his execution.

CHAPTER 2

Lenin

VLADIMIR ILYICH ULYANOV, later known as 'Lenin', was born into a bureaucratic middle class family in 1870 at Simbirsk. Ulyanov studied at Kazan University but, expelled for his political activities, completed his Law degree privately in 1891. He practised as a lawyer for a short time before moving to St Petersburg in 1894. Ulyanov was a natural object of suspicion to the authorities since his brother, Alexander, had been executed in 1887 for his part in a plot to assassinate the Tsar. A deep involvement in radical agitation and organization led to Ulyanov's exile in Siberia in 1897. The following year he married Nadezhda Konstantinovna Krupskaya. In 1900 Lenin moved to Switzerland and began to create a group which later coalesced around the journal *Iskra*. As the leader of the Bolshevik (majority) faction in the Russian Social Democratic Party he returned to Russia for two years after the attempted revolution of 1905. During World War I he called for workers to unite against the bloodshed but grew pessimistic about the prospects for revolution. In April, 1917, however, he was transported, by permission of the Germans, to Petrograd and in the same year seized power through a *coup d'état*. From 1918 to 1921 he consolidated his Party's hold on the country in the face of attempts by the White Armies which were attempting, with foreign support, to overthrow the Bolsheviks. In 1918 he bought peace by ceding large areas to the Germans by the Treaty of Brest-Litovsk. Realistically, he decided to allow some features of a mixed economy to continue for a while by his New Economic Policy (1922); in May of the same

19

year he suffered a stroke, another followed in December. On 21 January, 1924, he died at Gorki, his country home outside Moscow.

Few would question the inclusion of Vladimir Ilyich Ulyanov, Lenin, in a book on theories of revolutionary violence and war—yet Lenin did not come to power in such a war. His seizure of the reins of government was closer in form to a *coup d'état* than to a revolution. Nor had he been through a long period of armed struggle. His achievement, however, was little short of miraculous when one considers the position of the revolutionary parties in the Russia of 1914, a mere four years before the assumption of power.

Russia had gone into the First World War economically stronger than ever before. The reforms of Witte between 1892 and 1903, and Stolypin (1906–11) were beginning to bear fruit, even though both these Tsarist Ministers had been succeeded by lesser men. Between 1894 and 1914 gold reserves had increased dramatically (in 1894 they stood at 648,000,000 gold roubles, by 1914 this figure had risen to 1,604,000,000), the standard of living had doubled and savings were seven times as high. Strikes were usually successful in that they invariably led to increased wages. Workers showed by their reaction to the declaration of war in 1914 that they were ruled by patriotic instincts rather than by any grievance against the régime.

The Left in Russia was, by contrast, in disarray. Liberal constitutional Parties had been for some years gaining ground at the expense of the Socialist Revolutionaries and the Marxist Russian Social Democratic Party. Continued economic expansion and piecemeal political reform might have meant an end to revolutionary hopes. This situation could only be altered by some cataclysmic event, such as a sudden economic collapse—or by war. Once the first patriotic fervour had worn off a long conflict was likely to bring

20

depression and disillusion. Germany was Russia's best market and the Baltic her natural outlet. Cut off from the West, Russia must choke to death. To Lenin war was not an occasion for national unity and compromise: it was a favourable environment for revolution. He had the example of the disastrous Russo–Japanese War and the attempted revolution of 1905 to confirm him in his view; only then had violence seemed for a moment to hold promise of success. In 1915 Lenin made his position on the war very clear, through the statements which he and the 'Left' group at the Zimmerwald Conferences of socialist parties issued concerning their attitude to the conflict: 'Civil war between the classes, that is our slogan'—'Rise up and fight to end this slaughter'—'Turn your weapons against the common foe, the capitalist governments'.

In the end the Tsarist Government was not brought down by Lenin's Bolsheviks, armed or otherwise, but by its own failure to conduct the war efficiently. Suspicions of German sympathies at the Tsarist Court, the sinister influence of the monk Rasputin, and the breakdown of communication between Tsar and people left the way open for propagandists to turn worker and, crucially, soldier, against the Government.

The Provisional Government which attempted to rule the country after the Tsar's abdication could not long expect a weary people to go on fighting. All the eloquence of its leader, Kerensky, would be unable to prevent the one common desire—for 'Peace and Bread'—from becoming irresistible. Lenin knew it and was prepared to risk Russian humiliation, international contempt and civil war by giving the people what they wanted.

The Civil War duly came, but even then lacked the character of a revolutionary war since it was the defence of an existing Bolshevik Government against the attacks of the White Armies, led by ex-Tsarist Generals. The Whites were supported by foreign powers and thus the war had more the appearance of a national defence of 'Mother Russia' than of a revolutionary struggle. The Red Army which fought in that war was in any case the creation of Trotsky rather than Lenin. It was a positional, not a guerrilla war—not even by proxy did Lenin obtain any experience of irregular warfare. Certainly the Bolsheviks did have the support of guerrilla bands. Most remarkable was that led by Nestor Makhno—but Makhno was not even a Marxist, still less a Bolshevik. His campaigns were in the tradition of anarchist peasant uprisings against external authority and had nothing to do with Leninism.

Lenin's reputation as a theorist of armed revolution is nevertheless well deserved. He had a very clear picture of the role of violence in revolution. His theories and their swift application at the politically crucial moment provided a foundation on which others could build. The prestige attaching to his name meant that later theorists of revolutionary war were eager to lay claim to the title 'Leninist'. Formulations of revolutionary strategy which he produced after his assumption of power were naturally accorded immense respect. In fact Lenin was not an elegant theoretician but a political opportunist. He believed in the need for manœuvre and compromise; he followed the very un-Marxist concept of the intuitive grasp of the crucial moment to strike against the enemy ('lightning inspiration'—the Clausewitzian *Blitz des Geistes*).

Lenin's approach to the uses of violence, robbery and deceit was entirely amoral; all must be judged solely by the standard of political effectiveness. 'Expropriations' from banks, the diversion of funds from their intended destinations into Bolshevik coffers, the adoption and repetition of slogans which bolstered Lenin and denigrated his opponents —all were techniques supportive of one aim: the seizure and retention of power by a Leninist élite. So he stole the name *'Pravda'* from a successful journal of Trotsky's; similarly he appropriated the title *'Bolshevik'* ('the majority group') quite unjustifiably and succeeded in labelling the other faction in the Russian Social Democratic Party as

22

'*Menshevik*' ('the minority'). His agents married two sisters so that an inheritance could find its way into Party funds—though one of the agents had to be threatened before he would disgorge his gains. A bank robbery at Tiflis, which involved the youthful Stalin, produced 300,000 roubles and when they couldn't lay their hands on genuine bank notes, the Bolsheviks forged them. 'We should,' wrote Lenin, 'permit armed attacks for the purposes of seizing financial resources from the enemy . . . and for the purposes of armed uprising . . . under the Party's supervision.'[1] Lenin was not interested in Party unity as such, he was concerned only with the triumph of Leninism, though it must be said that in his mind the two amounted to the same thing. Since he refused to compromise his views in the interests of superficial unity, those who did always appeared to be prevaricating. Lenin became the incorruptible hard-liner and others *had their positions defined in relation to his.* The question to Lenin was always, 'Who, Whom?'; who is the subject, and who the object? Who defines the terms? Crudely—who is the 'doer' and who the 'done'?

Lenin said little that was new; the rich tradition of Russian revolutionary experience had offered most of the practicable (and many impracticable) alternatives already. It was because he said things more vehemently and lived them more completely than any of his contemporaries that he became the revolution personified; tough, uncompromising, dedicated. It was not what he said but the fact that *he* said it, that carried conviction.

Among the most important aspects of the Leninist emphasis in the theory of revolutionary violence are those concerning the role of the élite professional activists and the switching of the point of attack from advanced European to colonial countries. Lenin also extended the theory of violence into the post-revolutionary period when it could be used to eradicate all traces, human and physical, of the old régime.

Lenin stood at the junction of two revolutionary traditions. Total commitment and the use of the small dedicated élite were the hallmarks of the Russian populist terrorists who carried out a series of assassinations in the late nineteenth century, including that of Tsar Alexander II in 1881.[2]

Nechayev, a follower of the anarchist Bakhunin, and the model of Dostoyevsky's 'possessed', Peter Verkhovensky, was the archetypal terrorist. To Nechayev terrorism was aimed at smashing an evil order; from the ruins there would arise a new and natural society. Destruction would bring about the conditions for the emergence of a 'renewed personality'. Going to the masses was irrelevant, as they had demonstrated in 1874 when they had received with a sullen indifference the young Populist idealists who went among them. Sunk in apathy, the people needed awakening by the example of dramatic terrorist action. Martyrs, resolute and courageous even as the hangman placed a noose about their necks, must be provided as exemplars of revolutionary dedication; one such was Lenin's brother, Alexander Ulyanov, executed in 1887 for his part in a plot to assassinate the Tsar.

Contrasted with this populist tradition, but united with it in the person of Lenin, was the impressive theoretical consistency of Marxism. Certainty, persuasively based on a 'scientific' analysis of the economic basis of society, was thus added to fanaticism. To be a Russian Marxist at the turn of the century meant to be involved in abstruse arguments over the precise state of the development of society. The time did not, according to the theory, appear to be ripe for revolution since the Russian proletariat was too small and the bourgeoisie too weak to produce the conditions of class struggle foreseen by Marx. Germany was seen as most closely approximate to Marx's model and it was there that the nineteenth-century ideologues expected the revolution to occur. Some advocated an alliance with the bourgeoisie in Russia so that the feudal stage of Tsarist domination might the more quickly give way to the capitalist exploitation which would awaken the workers.

In exile in France, Germany, Britain and Switzerland the revolutionaries, riddled with mutual suspicion, fiddled and fumbled as they tried to unravel a series of ideological Gordian knots. Russia hardly noticed them—except for the Police spies who had infiltrated into their midst. Lenin knew that the only way to cut through this tangled verbiage was with the sword. Deeds, action, agitation on the basis of a Marxist analysis of when and where to strike—this was the way forward.

Lenin began to forge his sword between 1901 and 1903 with the formation of his own group, loyal to him personally, around the unifying symbol of the magazine *Iskra* (The Spark). His object was to create a small, reliable band of Leninists. There would be no flirting with the ideas of Bernstein, a German Marxist, who argued that the lot of the working class could best be improved through parliamentary institutions. 'Economism', the attempt to improve working conditions by piecemeal industrial action, would similarly be eschewed. Only the destruction of the existing order through violence, and the ensuing dictatorship of the proletariat, could ensure the true freedom of the working class. Tight central control was needed to avoid a haphazard approach (characterized by Lenin as *kustarnichestvo*—parochial disorganization).

After 1901 the *Iskraist* organization spread to link up with local committees inside Russia. During the succeeding years Lenin used his contacts to secure votes in Party Congresses. Thus he built up his own power base and organization. Despite his hard line on most issues he did not advocate terrorism *per se*; it was only an effective tactic if it was carefully co-ordinated with a political programme. It was left to the rival Socialist Revolutionaries, the organizational heirs of the populist revolutionary tradition, to carry on with the tactic of assassination. The Socialist Revolutionaries emphasized the essentially Russian nature of the problem facing the Left and rejected what they saw as irrelevant European models. It was the Socialist Revolutionaries, rather

25

than the Social Democrats, who first perceived the importance of the peasantry. 'Land' was a cry which touched a deep chord in the Russian heart; although Lenin initially rejected this approach he was later to use it to devastating effect. From 1902 to 1914, however, the Socialist Revolutionaries' analysis of the Russian situation was more accurate than that of either Bolshevik or Menshevik.

In underground organization and double-dealing intrigue Lenin was a genius. He also understood that nine-tenths of apparent genius is hard and unremitting work. Even if his organization should be largely destroyed he was determined that his reputation and methodology would survive. Thus he was able, though with difficulty, to overcome the later (1914) revelation that his most trusted lieutenant, Roman Malinovsky, was a police agent.

Lenin's language was frequently military in tone. He envisaged an organization as disciplined as that of an army and as fanatical as a secret brotherhood. He speaks of 'unity of view and singleness of will' . . . 'strictest discipline' . . . 'international capital' not being able to withstand the 'army of the proletariat' and so on. This is not surprising in view of Lenin's close acquaintance with the works of Clausewitz. Typically Lenin selected those aspects which accorded with his own ideas and ignored the rest. He adapted Clausewitz' philosophy of war *between* States to war *within* States and *between* classes. The revolutionary must see himself as *at war* with the State. 'The conqueror', remarked Clausewitz, 'is always peace-loving, since war comes from the resistance which the defender offers to his offensive'; this mordant observation drew from Lenin the marginal comment, 'Ha, ha, that's witty!'[3] It has remained a Communist tactic to blame any violence on the Government's 'criminal refusal' to surrender. Lenin continued to find confirmation for his views on the primacy of politics in the writings of the Prussian General and, as late as 1922, remarked that 'political tactics and military tactics are what the Germans call a *Grenzgebiet*' (overlapping area) and 'party workers would profit by studying thoroughly the works of the great German military theorist Clausewitz'.

Lenin's tactical ideas are to be found most notably in two works, *What Is To Be Done?* (1902) (with its postscript, *Letter to a Comrade on Our Organizational Tasks*) and *Lessons of the Moscow Uprising*. It must be emphasized that Lenin's main contribution is organizational: he calls consistently for flexibility not dogmatism. This is true both of his writings and his practice. 'Marxism,' he wrote, 'does not tie the movement to any particular combat method,' and he was as good as his word, for between the 'two revolutions' of 1917 he changed his tactics five times.

What Is To Be Done? (the title was copied from that of an earlier influential novel by Chernyshevsky) envisages a 'militant organization of agents'. Many organizations are needed, concedes Lenin, 'but it would be absurd and dangerous to confuse them with the organization of revolutionaries . . . We must have people who will devote themselves exclusively to activities . . . Such people must train themselves patiently and steadfastly to be professional revolutionaries.' Nor must these revolutionaries have any false pride: 'If you can't adjust yourself, if you won't crawl on your belly in the mud, then you're not a revolutionary but a chatterbox.'[4] There must be 'a centralization of the most secret functions in an organization of revolutionaries'. Whatever his rejection of spontaneous terrorism, he nevertheless argued that, once violence had commenced, terrorism must be used fully and ruthlessly. One of Lenin's biographers has called *What Is To Be Done?* an 'improved educated version of Nechayev's *Revolutionary Catechism* . . . Marxist Nechayevism'.[5]

In 1905 insurrection had broken out in Moscow; the authorities had reacted mercilessly, even using artillery, and the workers had been crushed. Plekhanov, the leading theorist of the older generation of exiled Marxists, suggested that 'they should not have taken up arms'; Lenin would have none of such defeatism. Once insurrection had begun, he said, all means should be used to further it. Every squad could learn in such a situation; Bolshevik duty was ruthlessly to exterminate civil and military leaders. Lenin gave detailed recommendations on tactics: the insurrectionaries could climb on roofs and throw stones and boiling water down on the troops; spies and policemen should be murdered and members of reactionary organizations dealt with—'beat them up, kill them, blow up their headquarters'. Those who shrank from such extreme measures were labelled 'quasi-democrats' and 'liberal chatterboxes'.[6] Elsewhere Lenin wrote that the Party must be like an Army, marching to victory by the shortest route; not words but revolutionary deeds were required.[7] Like Napoleon he adopted the motto: 'On s'engage et puis on voit.'

Later, in *State and Revolution* (August, 1917), Lenin was to praise Engels' panegyric on violent revolution: 'The State machinery must be shattered.' *State and Revolution* was meant to deal a blow both to reformists and anarchists. Parliamentary institutions, wrote Lenin, should be infiltrated, undermined and brought crashing down. They had to be replaced, however, by new organizations if counter-revolution was in its turn to be defeated. When Lenin achieved power he was determined not to repeat the errors of the Paris Commune of March to May, 1871, which, in his view, had been defeated because of 'the excessive magnanimity of the proletariat; it should have wiped out its enemies'.[8] In *State and Revolution* he made his views quite clear: 'Overthrow the capitalists, crush the resistance of these exploiters with the iron hand of the armed workers, break the bureaucratic machine of the contemporary State.'

· Lenin's second contribution to revolutionary theory was to switch the emphasis from Europe to the colonial world. When it became clear after 1918 that the rest of Europe was not going to follow the Russian example, the future of Marxist revolution seemed unclear. In Berlin, Bavaria and Hungary revolutionary expectations were disappointed and the Russian attempt to export revolution to Poland by force of arms was a dismal failure. Far from welcoming the Red Army the Polish workers fought resolutely against it. In the advanced industrial countries, where the contradictions of capitalism should have been most acute, the workers were turning, not to revolution, but to Trade Union and constitutional political activity. This seeming paradox was resolved by arguing, as had the Marxist writer Rosa Luxemburg (murdered in Berlin by men of the Cavalry Guards), that the workers of Europe had been bought off by a material well-being provided through colonial exploitation. A European aristocracy of labour had been created. Thus, said Lenin, the advanced European nations must be attacked at one remove, through their colonies; he had already, as early as 1908, noticed the tide of events, when he referred to the awakening of a whole series of bourgeois-democratic national movements. The capitalist edifice was founded on Empire and in the colonies revolution had millions of potential soldiers. Such a strategy would be a further generalization of the Russian experience in which Lenin had been able to use the frustrated aspirations of ethnic minorities to good effect (e.g. by attacking 'Great Russian Chauvinism' Lenin had achieved political advantages both locally and internationally; this could be repeated on a global scale with 'imperialism').

In 1919 Lenin suggested that the revolution in Asia might precede that in Europe; in 1920 he observed that, in giving weapons to colonial peoples and instructing them in their use, the West was digging its own grave. 'In the long run,' remarked Lenin (1923), 'capitalism itself is educating and training the vast majority of the world for the struggle.' To attack 'imperialism' had considerable propaganda advantages; 'self determination' was already a sacred phrase with liberals. It also conformed to the historical traditions of the United States of America which, in a common passion for national liberation movements, might be misled as to the ultimate aims of Communism.

Finally, the war against capitalism has to be continued

29

into the post-revolutionary period; there must be no chance of a come-back by the old régime. In *State and Revolution* (1917) Lenin defended the seizure of power and reiterated his views on violence. He had acted in a typically opportunist fashion and his constant changes of policy seemed impossible to justify in Marxist terms. Hence there was an ideological need for explanation. The State must, he argued, be destroyed and this could only be brought about by violence; nothing else could provide a sufficiently clean break with the past. The Party must ruthlessly and utterly wipe the slate clean: 'terror', said Dzerzhinsky, Lenin's Secret Police Chief, 'is an absolute necessity during times of revolution.'

We have seen that Lenin devised a technique for the leadership of a large number of organizations (some openly Communist, some co-operating with 'progressive elements', some covert) by a disciplined core of professionals. Thus the 'command staff' of the revolution would co-ordinate all activities in order to achieve the political aim. This approach was, in principle, of universal application, though needing careful application to the conditions of colonial countries, where so much revolutionary potential was concentrated. Once revolution *as an act* had occurred, it had to be continued *as a process*. The counter-revolution must be decapitated.

Pervading all his tactical thought is Lenin's grasp of the importance of the war of words. Mastery of propaganda, and the destruction of the enemy's ability to communicate with the people, is essential. He quoted approvingly from Napoleon's *Pensées*—'the cannon killed feudalism, ink will kill modern society'. Lenin faced a ruthless and sophisticated enemy in the Tsarist Russian Secret Police, which infiltrated revolutionary organizations, ran Trade Unions and even carried out terrorist acts (not excepting assassinations) in order to bolster the reputation of its operatives or to make propaganda. Through Malinovsky, the Police even paid and used Lenin himself. His hard line had the virtue, in police eyes, of splitting the Russian Social Democratic Party still further into an ineffective factionalism. Lenin fought fire with fire. Believing in the infallibility of Leninism, he saw no wrong in stealing funds as well as slogans, even from fellow-Marxists, and in employing criminals in his organizations. All were useful in fighting the total war against the Government which Lenin envisaged. 'This isn't a school for young ladies,' he said; to prove it he proceeded to use Victor Taratuta (later a *Comintern* agent) because he was an 'intelligent crook'.

Ultimately the battle was one of perception, propaganda and persuasion; Lenin feared the enemy's propaganda more than his cruder oppressions. Martyrs were useful; to be made to look foolish was a disaster. In an extraordinary outburst to Gorky in 1913 Lenin warned of the dangers of using 'God-substitutes' instead of anathematizing all religion:

> The Catholic priest who deflowers young girls (I happen to have been reading about one just now) is *far* less of a danger to 'democracy' than a priest without a cassock, a priest without a crude religion, an intellectual, democratic priest preaching the building and creation of dear little gods.[9]

It was to be the use of the propaganda of 'Peace, Bread and Land' which in the end maintained in power a ruthless Bolshevik minority after its *putsch*.

Leninism is an exercise in political psychology, and violence is an essential part of its armoury.

NOTES

1 Quoted Shukman, *Lenin and the Russian Revolution*, Batsford, London, 1966, p 102
2 Karl Marx himself expressed great admiration for the populist

31

terrorists of *Narodnaya Volya* (People's Will); see McLellan, *Karl Marx, His Life and Thought*, Macmillan, 1973, p 441. As for Lenin, 'he considered violence a legitimate, indeed a preferred method and advocated it coldly, openly'. (Fischer, Louis, *Lenin*, Weidenfeld & Nicolson, London, 1965)

3   See Keep, John, in *Lenin; the Man, the Theorist, the Leader*, Pall Mall, 1967, especially pp 135–58, for Lenin's understanding of Clausewitz

4   Lenin at the 7th Party Congress, March, 1918

5   Possony, Stefan T., *Lenin*, George Allen & Unwin, London, 1966, p 79

6   Marx's approving quotation of Georges Sand reflects a similar view: 'On the eve of every general re-structuring of society, the last word of social science will always be: Le combat ou la mort, la lutte sanguinaire ou le néant. C'est ainsi que la question est invinciblement posée.' McLellan, op cit, p 165

7   See Lenin, *Selected Works*, Moscow, 1950, Vol. I, p 110

8   Speech on the 37th anniversary of the Paris Commune, 18 March, 1908

9   Shukman, op cit, p 131

CHAPTER 3

Trotsky

LEV DAVIDOVICH BRONSTEIN (TROTSKY) was born at
Yanovka in the Ukraine in 1877. Educated privately and
in Nikolaev and Odessa, he mixed with populist
revolutionaries and became acquainted with Marxism.
After a period of exile in Siberia he went to London and
there met Lenin (1902). In 1905 he achieved fame for his
part in organizing and running the first Soviet in
St Petersburg. Trotsky turned his trial for his 1905 activity
into a personal triumph, escaped from his subsequent
Siberian exile and lived (from 1907 to 1914) in Vienna.
On the outbreak of the war he fled to Zurich and then to
France, from which he was deported in 1916. For a while
he lived in America and, in 1917, after frustrating delays,
managed to reach Petrograd. As Commissar for Foreign
Affairs he headed the Russian delegation to Brest-Litovsk.
In 1918 he became Commissar for War and created the
Red Army. After Lenin's death in 1924 Trotsky was
unable—and apparently unwilling—to match Stalin in
political machination. Expelled from Russia in 1929 he
sought refuge in various countries, eventually being
granted asylum in Mexico. Condemned to death *in
absentia* by a Soviet court, Trotsky was assassinated by a
Stalinist agent in 1940.

'Trotsky was at that time extraordinarily elegant, in contrast to all of us, and very handsome. This elegance of
his, and especially a sort of carelessly condescending
manner of speaking to no matter who struck me very

disagreeably. With great malevolence I looked at this dandy, with one leg slung over the other, dashing off with a pencil an outline of an impromptu speech.'

The above quotation (from Lunacharsky, later Soviet Commissar for Education) goes some way to explaining the fascination which Trotsky's memory still holds.[1] It is not merely that the revelations of Stalin's cruelties have served to increase the reputation of his opponents nor that the efforts of Soviet ideologues to cast Trotsky into the outer darkness have been so clumsily counter-productive.[2] Trotsky can still inspire revolutionaries today because he was a truly international figure. The very characteristics which weakened him in his struggle with Stalin have ensured the survival of his ideas.

In the West the Left wing tends to be intellectual and cosmopolitan: so was Trotsky. 'Repression' is seen today as more than a physical phenomenon; alone among the Russian revolutionaries, Trotsky had some understanding of Freud. Since the revolutionary Left in the West seems nowhere close to victory it tends to play with grand theory. Writing and speech-making are substituted for organizational drudgery. Trotsky was the most eloquent journalist and the greatest orator produced by the Russian Revolution. Since Trotsky was so soon a voice in the wilderness his memory did not become contaminated by the deportations and forced collectivization of the Stalinist era. Trotsky was able to criticize without the responsibility of decision. The fact that his name was used simply to smear anybody Stalin's *apparatchiks* disliked later redounded to Trotsky's credit. The bitter absurdity that thousands of people died as 'Trotskyist agents' in Stalin's purges ensured a resurrection for Trotsky, even as it guaranteed the butcher's reputation to Stalin himself.

Moreover, on a number of crucial issues Trotsky was proved correct; over the strategy towards China in the 1920s and in his attitude to the dangers of 'socialism in one (Russian) country' taking precedence over 'world-wide revolution' it was Trotsky not Stalin who has been vindicated by history. Under Stalin the Communist International, founded by Trotsky and Lenin, rapidly became, as the former had feared, merely an alternative instrument of Russian foreign policy. Trotsky's condemnation of 'Great Russian Chauvinism' was remembered when Soviet tanks rumbled through the streets of Budapest in 1956 and Prague in 1968. In the West the 'new Left', equally disgusted with Russian as with American 'imperialism', found in Trotsky a prophet, in the true apostolic succession of revolution, with whom they could identify. Through him they could see themselves, rather than the Stalinists, as the heirs of the revolutionaries of 1789, 1848, 1905 and 1917. Trotsky, it seemed, had kept alive the flame of revolution through the dark night of Stalinism. As he grew more popular, and books, plays and films about him grew more numerous, so the Soviet propaganda machine unwittingly increased Trotsky's notoriety by the virulence of its attacks.

Trotsky's revolutionary theory also seemed peculiarly appropriate to the division between the 'third world' and the advanced capitalist countries. The theory of 'permanent revolution' appeared to be supported by the realities of the 1960s. Capitalism could plausibly be seen as on the point of collapse. The system of nation states was finding great difficulty in coping with the challenges of the multi-national corporation on the one hand and associations of raw material producers on the other. The concept of a 'world of sovereign states' seemed to be less and less relevant to the realities of global power. If the system *was* on the point of collapse, what should take its place? Trotskyists claimed that they knew the causes, had the means to interpret and predict the process, and would finally see the triumph of world revolution. Trotsky's reputation emerged from all this not merely restored but glamourized.

If Trotsky's humanity has somehow been lost between the conflicting representations of him as beast or hero, his view of revolutionary violence remains important if only in the secondary sense that many people study it and some believe in it; in any other sense it can be seen as anachronistic.

Trotsky saw violence as an integral part of the process of revolution but he did not believe that terrorism alone could create the conditions for such a revolution. He had observed that, far from demonstrating the nature of despotism, the assassination of Tsar Alexander II had appeared to many Russians as the vengeance of the gentry on the 'protector of the peasants'. The violence of the Socialist Revolutionaries seemed to him counter-productive and he was perhaps the most outspoken of the revolutionary leaders in its condemnation. In 1912 Trotsky wrote that individualist terrorism was inadmissible precisely because it downgraded the role of the masses in their own consciousness, led them to accept their own powerlessness and turned their eyes and hopes towards a 'great avenger and liberator' who would some day come and accomplish his mission.

Once the revolution had begun, however, terrorism became essential. Trotsky's experience of the abortive revolution of 1905 convinced him of the necessity of the workers possessing weapons; 'the unarmed heroism of the crowd', as he put it, 'cannot face the armed idiocy of the barracks.'

There are two aspects to Trotsky's approach to revolution which concern us here: the general theory of *permanent revolution* and, at a more pragmatic level, the tactical details based on his experiences of 1905 and 1917.

Trotsky's concept of *permanent revolution* referred to the dimensions both of Time and Space. As regards Russia it would be impossible, because of the weakness of the bourgeoisie, to prevent the revolution proceeding directly to socialism. Either reaction or revolution would triumph; there was no possibility of some half-way house of bourgeois democracy. 'In a country economically backward', wrote Trotsky, 'the proletariat can take power earlier than in countries where capitalism is advanced . . . the Russian revolution produces conditions in which power may pass into the hands of the proletariat before the politicians of bourgeois liberalism have had the chance to show their statesman-like genius to the full.' In the early 1900s this aspect of the theory of permanent revolution seemed to fly in the face of Marxist orthodoxy and of reasonable expectation.

Not only could the revolution be fulfilled more quickly, but also more widely. Trotsky saw the revolution as an international phenomenon, to which national boundaries were irrelevant. If, later, General Giap was to see international and foreign tensions as aiding an existing national revolution, Trotsky had already, in 1905, perceived the obverse of that coin. National revolutions were also initiated by international problems. Revolution in any one country might be the result of pressures applied to it via the international system.

In urging this view of revolution as an international process Trotsky had been influenced by the writings of Alexander Israel Helphand, better known by the pen-name 'Parvus.' Social tensions capable of producing revolution were present all over the world; Russia might be the first to exhibit the violent results of such tensions . . . but its example would spark off a chain reaction elsewhere—so ran the argument. Thus Trotsky expected that the 1917 Russian experience would prove to be merely the vanguard of an integrated European revolution. There would be one process of insurrection and emancipation which would lead naturally to the ending of global imperialism. While the revolution must start within one nation it cannot, claimed Trotsky, be finished there. Militarily and economically European States were interdependent, they would inevitably seek to co-operate in order to crush the revolution. Therefore the revolution must take steps to weaken, divide and ultimately replace the Governments of such States.

Revolution was thus presented as an alternative world order. Revolutionaries owed their allegiance only to one another and to the hidden revolutionary counter-system. This vision was bold, imaginative and impracticable. Workers of the world, far from uniting, did one another to death in their millions after 1914. Socialists became chauvinists overnight. Trotsky, however, never lost his vision or his belief. He remained consistent. In his attitude to Zionism, for example, he insisted that not in the formation of yet another nation-state would the Jews find their emancipation but in the changed values of a new international society.

Trotsky's tactics of revolutionary struggle were realistic and pragmatic. He refused to be bound by the restrictions of Marxist orthodoxy. The licensed practitioners of Marxist interpretation, like so many soothsayers constantly examining the entrails for signs and portents, seemed to him merely ridiculous. Marxism, he asserted, was a method of analysing, not sacred texts, but social relationships. Many years later he was to quote approvingly from Clausewitz: 'One should not drive the flowers and the foliage of theory too high—one should rather keep them close to the soil of experience.'

Despite the virulence of his journalistic attacks on Lenin's ideas of an élite of professional revolutionaries, Trotsky agreed with the need for central direction and control. He warned of the dangers of 'substitutism', i.e. that the Party Organization will forget the Party, that the Central Committee will ignore the Party Organization and that a dictator will finally run all of them. On the other hand he had admitted in 1901 that there must be a Central Committee with power to discipline any unruly organization or individual.

The support of the peasantry was seen by Trotsky as important to the success of the revolution. Although the lead was taken by the proletariat and the town would be the main centre of action, the peasantry should rapidly be involved. In the 1920s Trotsky, almost alone of the Russian leaders, was to urge the need for peasant activity in China.

Trotsky's experience led him to emphasize the crucial importance of the revolutionaries' seizure of arms. In 1907 Trotsky, according to the dossier in the French Police

Archives, attributed the failure of the 1905 revolution to the fact that the Russian Prime Minister Stolypin 'had the Army on his side'. It was necessary therefore, concluded Trotsky, 'to conduct active propaganda in the Army'.[3] If Trotsky's main revolutionary weapon, the General Strike, was to succeed, it must be defended with arms. At the same time efforts to use the Armed Forces either to intimidate the workers or to take over any of their tasks must be resisted. The way to achieve these aims was to turn the city into an armed camp. At the moment of confrontation between Army and strikers the years of agitation and propaganda in the barracks would finally pay off. The barricade, suggested Trotsky, was principally the physical and moral meeting ground between the people and the Army. If they have been properly prepared by agents within the Army, the soldiers will refuse to oppose the striking workers and may even go over to their side. A contemporary observer wrote that Trotsky knew how to capture the man behind the machine-gun, instead of merely countering him with another gun.[4] In any case groups of armed workers must stand up to the troops and force them to choose between shooting and refusing to obey orders. 'We must develop the most intense agitation among the troops', wrote Trotsky, 'so that at the moment of the (General) strike every soldier sent to suppress the "rebels" should know that in front of him is the people.'[5] The failure of the revolution of 1905 was partly due to the fact that the largely peasant Army, which was itself not disaffected against the Government until after the moment of confrontation, was faced by an unarmed proletariat. A General Strike cannot be carried on for ever; either it will result in the overthrow of the Government or it will fizzle out as hunger and despair drive men back to work.

If the disaffection of the Armed Forces was to be effective it needed to be combined with a seizure of the technological nerve centres of the State apparatus. In particular rail and telecommunications links should be used to organize the

39

revolution rather than being available to its opponents. By having rail, post and telegraph workers on the side of the revolution one might hope to unite all the revolutionary strongpoints of the country with the 'steel of rails and telegraph wire'. It was not only the armed forces which would be subverted. During Tsardom's partial recovery after 1907 Trotsky urged the importance of infiltrating all the institutions recognized by the State—Parliament, Trade Unions and the professions as well as the military. Trotsky expressed these points with his usual eloquence in an open letter to the Liberal politician Miliukov:

An historical Rubicon is truly crossed . . . when the material means of government pass from the hands of absolutism into those of the people . . . such things . . . take place on the street and are achieved through struggle.[6]

As the Government collapsed so the revolutionaries would have available another 'government' (a 'parallel hierarchy') to step into its shoes.

It is at this point that terrorism, the decapitation of the counter-revolution, becomes important. During this period the 'class will of the enemy' must be broken by the 'systematic and energetic use of violence'; terrorism kills individuals and intimidates thousands.[7]

Trotsky's theory of permanent revolution led naturally to an emphasis on the colonial world. If the expected revolution in Europe did not in fact materialize then the main focus of effort should be transferred elsewhere. History, remarked Trotsky, had moved along the lines of least resistance. The revolutionary age had entered through the least barricaded gates: on 5 August, 1919, in a secret memorandum to the Central Committee, Trotsky suggested that those gates lay in Asia.

For Trotsky the conquest of power by the proletariat does not complete the revolution but only opens it. It would be, he suggested, essential to defend the revolution against three enemies in particular. Since the revolution would succeed well before most of the people had become 'proletarians' there would be the danger of a reaction led by remnants of the old régime. The peasant class could be expected to fight collectivization tooth and nail and, finally, the foreign powers would certainly attempt to terminate a process which might threaten them too. The destruction of the new Soviet Government and the restoration of the old Tsarism or a bourgeois government would be a natural concern of 'capitalist Europe'.

To Trotsky fell the task of meeting these challenges by creating a Red Army. While Trotsky's organization was brilliant it involved the sacrifice of a number of his own principles. The very success which he enjoyed aroused jealousies and a suspicion of 'Bonapartism', i.e. that Trotsky would use the weapon he had forged to bolster his own power. No accusation could have been wider of the mark. When the Civil War was won it was Trotsky who urged the replacement of the standing Red Army by a People's Militia. He was opposed by the Generals, especially Tukhachevsky and Svechin, who stood out for a professional Army.

Influenced by Clausewitz' emphasis on the moral factor in war, Trotsky argued that the revolution could only be continued and defended by an army integrated with the people. He wanted the standing army to give way to a militia organized on a factory/collective farm basis. To him the Red Army was an interim organization brought about by the necessities of the Civil War. Party and Government, he urged, must together commit themselves to the militia as the final objective of policy. This view, it must be emphasized, was integral to Trotsky's revolutionary theory since it linked with his outlook on the global nature of revolution. Military professionals, wishing to preserve their own institutions and status, argued for the use of the Red Army as 'an instrument of revolution'. In their view the Red Army could impose 'revolution by conquest' (which, to those imposed upon, felt no different from Tsarist Imperialism). The manifest absurdity of this proposition was not lost on Trotsky but he found himself involved in polemics to defend his opinion. Professional military opposition to militias sprang from the fact that they were exclusively defensive bodies, ill adapted to coercing foreigners into supporting the (Russian) Revolution. Trotsky's preoccupation with militias on the other hand was a natural continuation of his strategy of infiltrating the army of his opponents before the seizure of power. Unless arms remained in the hands of 'the people' (which could only be ensured by militia organizations) they might once more become 'instruments of oppression'. The potential for violence must remain under the control of the revolution.

There are of course inconsistencies in Trotsky's writings which, like Lenin's, were composed during the stress of rapidly changing events. His ideas constantly outran his, or anybody else's ability to put them into practice. There is some justification in the gibe of a modern Soviet writer who claims that Trotsky appeals to those who like him (and in Lenin's words), 'easily go to revolutionary extremes' but are 'incapable of perseverance, organization, discipline or steadfastness'.[8] He underrated both the apathy of the masses (as Lenin's wife, Krupskaya, suggested) and the power of nationalism; the Red Army, flung back from the gates of Warsaw by the fierce patriotism of the Poles in 1920 was to discover the latter for itself.[9]

It remains true, however, that Trotskyism is technically the best equipped theory for effecting a revolution in the modern world. Unlike Moscow-line Communist Parties (which anyway have generally abandoned any open commitment to 'revolution') Trotskyists cannot be accused of being the agents of a foreign power.[10] The patient and steady infiltration of institutions (especially the Armed Forces) and professions over the years will bear fruit at the moment of decisive confrontation, the General Strike.

Fortunately for those who support the present system of

Western democracy the Trotskyists in their midst have been unable to back this potential with any concerted action. Divided into squabbling factions and prone to arid doctrinal controversy, they have lacked the consistent application to detailed organizational work which alone could bring them real influence. Nor have they been able to produce locally credible leaders; many of their activists come from minority out-groups in the society in which they operate. Frequently they fail to understand the continuing strength of national and ethnic loyalties and still 'underrate the apathy of the masses'.

On the other hand it would be equally foolish for Governments to underrate *them*.

NOTES

1 The quotation also suggests a weakness which his enemies could exploit; Trotsky had a very unproletarian characteristic—style

2 The same comment might be made of Western writers; the propaganda picture drawn by Churchill was so extravagant that it served to increase rather than diminish its subject's reputation: 'Trotsky . . . sits disconsolate—a skin of malice stranded for a time on the shores of the Black Sea and now washed up in Mexico . . . like the cancer bacillus he grew, he fed, he tortured, he slew in fulfilment of his nature' (W. S. Churchill, *Great Contemporaries*, Thornton Butterworth, London, 1937)

3 Quoted in *Trotsky*, ed Smith, Irving H., Prentice Hall, 1973, p 55

4 Sir Lewis Namier in *The New Europe*, London, 1918

5 Deutscher, Isaac, *The Prophet Armed*, London, 1954, p 112

6 Deutscher, op cit, p 120

7 Trotsky, *Terrorism and Communism*, Ann Arbor, 1961, p 55

8 Basmanov in *Communist Viewpoint*, vol 2, no 3, 1970, Progress Books, Canada

9 A later Red Army was to meet a similar response in the Finland of 1939

10 Although, for tactical reasons, they may from time to time support and act for a foreign Government

CHAPTER 4

Fascist Theorists

In popular usage 'fascism' has become a smear word; it is a term of general abuse applied to people with whose opinions the speaker disagrees. By successfully equating 'fascism' with 'reaction' the Left has succeeded in giving the impression that it is in tune with the future, while its opponents are labelled as regressive.

Equally it can be argued that fascism[1] represents an historical tradition as old as that which is currently and partially reflected by communism. To prefer tradition, nation or race to class solidarity is not necessarily reactionary nor is there any reason why the latter should be morally more acceptable than the former. Even in its more bizarre manifestations fascism has been matched by some of the expressions of its communist *alter ego*. A Nazi 'Aryan soul' is no more mystical a concept than a 'proletarian soul'; the unnatural adoption of working class manners by the bourgeoisie is no less ridiculous than the striking of 'correct racial attitudes', and each springs from similar feelings of inadequacy, guilt and fear. Both communist and fascist used love and hatred to motivate their followers: love of one's class or nation, hatred of the Jews or the 'class enemy'. Even internationally there are striking similarities; the Nazis sought also to appeal *across* national boundaries to a higher unity of race, the Communists seek to appeal across national boundaries to the higher unity of class. Both denounced elections as fraudulent and both are equally subversive of a system based on sovereign nation states. Nor is fascism dead; ethnic minorities are as likely to turn to a type of fascism as to Marxist-Leninism. In Belgium Flemish and Walloon separatism has been fascist in the past and Basque nationalism in Spain has only recently taken on a specifically

Marxist–Leninist flavour. The precursors of the *Provisional IRA* (notwithstanding the socialist tone of many of its contemporary political statements) were the Irish fascist 'Blue Shirts' who sent a contingent to fight on Franco's side in the Spanish Civil War. Separatist movements are likely to embrace that ideology which offers the greatest chance of foreign support: Fascism in the days of Mussolini and Hitler, Communism in the days of Stalin and anti-colonialism if a Gaddafi of Libya might be tempted to assist.

Fascism, even granting the many varieties which it took, did display a sufficient unity of background and purpose to be considered a general *movement*. Moreover since its followers sought to change, and in some cases did change, the structure of their societies, it can be accounted a *revolutionary movement*. Fascism demanded radical social reforms, although more strongly in eastern Europe and in Spain than in Italy and Germany.[2] Fascism aimed at the overthrow of the existing order, its institutions and way of life and the creation of new structures, headed by a new élite. The fact that power was taken legally[3] (even if the opposition had been cowed by a systematic display of violence) does not invalidate the fascist claim to be revolutionary. A government democratically elected by a people with freedom of speech and association was to be replaced by a corporate state, with the final decision in the hands of the Leader. State and Party were to become synonymous. Old élites might retain their status but the price was total subservience to the orders of their new masters, the majority of whom were regarded as inferior in birth, education and morals.

Nor were fascist movements merely nationalistic in their ideologies and aims. Hitler and Mussolini sought more than an extension of German and Italian power and influence. To Hitler the imposition of a new world order, to Mussolini the creation of a Roman Empire, were the ultimate visions which inspired. Such irrational and grandiose objectives could not reasonably be regarded as being 'in the national interest'.

45

Both in revolutionary tactics and in ideology fascism in general and Nazism in particular made a distinct contribution to revolutionary theory.

Violence, while tactically crude, was used strategically with some subtlety. Displayed in meetings and on the streets, the objective of violence was to strike fear into opponents and overawe the bystanders. People were to be persuaded that the violence they saw, though frightening, was essentially a defence of values which were threatened by worse and less disciplined forces from the Left. Aliens, vague and mysterious, were poised to take over; opposition to the fascists was both dangerous and unpatriotic. A comforting identity was to be found in supporting fascism, only 'outsiders' fought against it. Thus while the Communist revolutionaries talked of strikes, arming the workers and guerrilla warfare, the fascists used force simply as a means of display. The propaganda of fist, boot and uniform exaggerated the size and influence of fascism. Fighting in the streets, rioting in the universities and brawling in political meetings showed up the weakness of the democracies. 'No intelligent man', asserted the Flemish leader, Van Severen, 'still believes in democracy'.[4] Such Governments were all too often not only supine but also corrupt.[5] Fascists admitted that their methods were crude but at least they were 'open and honest'.

Fascism led inexorably to the ultimate violence . . . war. Mussolini welcomed war; he had learnt from Lenin that war was the prime vehicle of revolutionary change. Fascist movements saw war as a means of regaining lost territories or lost peoples.[6]

Violence required a readily available source of disciplined manpower. Most fascist movements contained at least one élite militant group, and sometimes a hierarchy of them headed by the Leader's personal bodyguard.[7]

If violence was to achieve a public impact disproportionate to the Party's real strength it had to be ubiquitous as well as dramatic. Uniformed groups were moved swiftly from town to town and meeting to meeting (as early as 1922 the Nazis were purchasing trucks for this purpose). The media (whether the sophisticated apparatus of radio and newspaper or the mere retailing of village gossip) were exploited to give an illusion of pervasive power. Codreanu's Legionaries with white crosses on their breasts and turkey feathers in their caps galloping from one Rumanian village to another inspired the same kind of legendary awe which in a different society was symbolized by Hitler's travel by aeroplane and Goebbels' wireless propaganda.

At some point, however, the Party militias (*Sturmabteilung*,[8] Legionaries, Black Shirts etc) would come into conflict with those who were licensed to use force: the Police and the Army. Hitler, Mussolini and Franco came to terms with this crisis; others failed to realize the importance of gaining the support of the forces of law and order . . . and paid the penalty.

Hitler was ultimately successful in appealing, in the humiliating aftermath of the First World War, to the ex-servicemen's organizations such as the *Stahlhelm*.

The original Italian *fasci* ('organs of creation and agitation, capable of descending into the streets . . . men who forced the country into war and into victory') were formed round the Italian commando *arditi*. Ex-officers were prominent in the fascist movement from the beginning and maintained their contacts with their former colleagues in the Army. 'Long Live Italy! Long Live the King!' and, significantly, 'Long Live the Army' were the watchwords of the fascist 'March on Rome' of October, 1922. In the north in particular the Army co-operated with the Fascists. The Rome garrison could have stopped the March but the King, fearful of bloodshed and assured by his generals that the Fascists had an overwhelming numerical superiority, gave way and invited Mussolini to become Prime Minister. The Blackshirt militia soon acquired legal status and, by swearing allegiance to the King, became part of the forces of the Italian State.

THE FASCIST TRADITION

Country	Main Movement	Leader	Para-Military Group	Influence (approximately)
BELGIUM				
(1) *Flanders*	Flemish Front/League of Netherlands National Solidarists	Joris van Severen	Green Shirt Militia	1919–1940
	VNV (Vlaamsch Nationaal Verbond)	Staf de Clercq		1933–1945
(2) *Wallonia*	Rex Party	Leon Degrelle		1936–1945
FINLAND	Lapua Movement/People's Patriotic Movement	Vilho Annala		1929–1941
FRANCE	Action Française	Charles Maurras	Camelots du Roi	1899–1919[1]
GERMANY	National Socialism	Adolf Hitler	*SS* and *SA*	1920–1945[2]
HUNGARY	Arrow Cross	Ferencz Szalasi		1935–1945
ITALY	Fascism	Benito Mussolini	Black Shirts	1919–1945
RUMANIA	Legion of Archangel Michael/Iron Guard	Ion Codreanu	Legionary Police	1927–1941

48

RUSSIA	Union of the Russian People	Dr A. I. Dubrovin	Yellow Shirts	1905–1913
SPAIN	Falange	Primo de Rivera	Blueshirts	1934–1936[3]
UNITED KINGDOM	British Union of Fascists	Sir Oswald Mosley	Blackshirts	1932–1939

[1] After 1919 Action Française was conservative rather than extreme Right Wing
[2] Austria had its National Socialists too and, in addition, the Heimwehr of Dr Walter Pfrimer which had influence from 1927 to 1934
[3] In 1937 the movement was taken over by the conservative *caudillo* Franco; it ceased to be simply fascist and took its ideology and aims from Franco as leader who used it to prop his régime

Hitler learned the importance of infiltrating the forces of the State through the failure of his *putsch* in November, 1923. The Army was against him and the Police fired on him. For him there was no Italian style 'march on Berlin'. As he moved away from political radicalism and sought an arrangement with German industrialists and businessmen[9] so it became necessary to control the activities of the *SA* more closely. Eventually Hitler was to dismember the *SA* (in favour of the more élite *SS*, originally his personal body-guard) by eliminating its leaders on the 'night of the long knives'.[10] The eclipse of the *SA* went some way towards allaying the fears of the professional Army, although in fact the *SS* was to prove a much more deadly rival.

From 1923 onwards Hitler realized the need to woo the German Army and Police. It was fruitless simply to oppose them as the arm of a discredited Government; they must be offered an alternative future, of high status, as the respected guardians of the law and security of the German *volk*. The policy of eastward expansion outlined in *Mein Kampf*[11] could only be carried out with the support and expertise of the German military establishment. During his trial after the November *putsch* Hitler made constant reference to the Army. 'The old flags will lead the way again . . . one day the hour will come when the *Reichswehr* will be standing at our side . . . officers and men.' Initially it was the younger officers who were attracted to Hitler's National Socialism. By 1929 lieutenants were issuing leaflets and suggesting that some units would support a Nazi seizure of power. Hitler, giving evidence at the trial of some of the young officers, promised grimly that the humiliation of November, 1918, would be avenged when the National Socialists triumphed. Once in power Hitler's policy of re-armament and expansion of the Armed Forces kept them on his side.

The early excesses of Hitler's followers in Munich were not checked because the Police were infiltrated by his supporters and leading officials Wilhelm Frick and Ernst Poehner sympathized with him. The Police did not move to suppress the Nazis; Nazi material was not censored and complaints against them were not followed up. Without the acquiescence of the Police, Hitler's movement could not have survived; the Führer admitted the debt and showed his gratitude by honouring Frick.[12]

Failure to persuade the Army to the side of fascism resulted everywhere in defeat. Codreanu's Iron Guard was not supported by the Army which preferred the alternative authoritarianism of King Carol and, later, General Antonescu. The Legion continued to exist until 1941; in that year the government, backed by the Army and by Hitler, easily defeated the amateur militias of the legionaries.

In Spain fascism was absorbed by the Army, rather than the reverse. Franco was no revolutionary, but a conservative *caudillo*. Removing any radical tendencies, he used a remodelled Falange to buttress his own régime.

Given the immense power which military forces possess today, the tactics of the fascist revolutionaries are not without interest; the revolutionary Left is usually totally anti-militarist and talks interminably about 'arming the workers'.[13] Today the revolution which persuades the armed forces on to its side may succeed, while that which abuses them will surely fail.

The classic elements of fascist ideology maintain their appeal.[14] Anti-semitism is not dead. The unemployed and poor may still blame their plight on those of different race, nation, religion or class. Fascism, like Communism, appeals to the desperate since it offers a simple explanation: evilly intentioned conspiracies are the culprits, motivated by racial origin (or class interest) and given scope for exploitation by the weak liberalism of democratic governments.

In contemporary Europe the extreme Left with its greater intellectual sophistication and foreign support poses the main threat to Western democracies: it is more numerous, more vocal, more subtle and better organized.

However the fascist tradition lives on; should a new leadership appear, intellectually able to maintain a wider

51

appeal based on an updated ideology, then any country with a stagnant economy will be under threat.

NOTES

1 Strictly speaking 'fascism' refers to Mussolini's Italian movement; more loosely it covers all those groups which sought to glorify allegedly ancient racial traditions against their enemies (Bolshevism and 'big business', especially when dominated by Jews). In this chapter 'fascism' will be used in the looser sense
2 Even in Italy the election slogan of 1919 was 'squeeze the rich'
3 In Germany by a decree of 28 February, 1933, abolishing the democratic freedoms and then by the Enabling Act, passed by the new Parliament elected in March, 1933: voting was 441 to 94. The fascist takeover in Italy was gradual, involving a series of laws passed mainly between 1923 and 1926
4 For this and generally see *The European Right*, ed Rogger and Weber, Weidenfeld & Nicolson, London, 1965
5 Corruption scandals in the Weimar government, for example, involving Jewish financiers, played into the hands of the Nazis
6 e.g. Fiume for Italy, the Sudetenland for Germany, Karelia for the Finns and Transylvania for the Hungarians
7 *Action Française* had its *camelots du roi*, Mussolini and Mosley their Blackshirts, Hitler the *SA* and *SS*
8 Originally 'bouncers' at political meetings, they were later given a uniform and reorganized under Captain Roehm in 1925; a good brief account is in Hanser, Richard, *Prelude to Terror*, Hart-Davis, London, 1971
9 e.g. at the Hamburg address, February, 1922; industrialists in the Ruhr were soon contributing to Party funds
10 30 June, 1934; the *SS* (*Schutz Staffel*) grew out of the *Stosstrup Hitler*
11 Written in prison April–December, 1924
12 He became Minister of the Interior and later Protector of Bohemia and Moravia
13 In Europe this is simply a mindless slogan repeated from old pamphlets, it has no practical *revolutionary* content
14 The emotional pulls of nature and instinct as against cold intellect, blood and soil as against arid logic, are likely to be eternally susceptible to political manipulation; see Mosse, George L., *The Crisis of German Ideology: Intellectual Origins of the Third Reich*, Weidenfeld & Nicolson, London, 1966

CHAPTER 5

Mao Tse-tung

MAO TSE-TUNG (1893–1976) was born in December 1893 in Hunan into a peasant family. He was formally educated at Changsha but learnt most during his time as an assistant librarian at the University of Peking (1918). Mao worked for a time as a schoolmaster and in 1921 became a founder member of the Chinese Communist Party. The failure of the Stalin-inspired policy of co-operation with Chiang Kai-shek's Nationalists and the crushing of Communist uprisings led Mao to consider the revolutionary potential of the peasantry with whom he worked closely from 1925 to 1927. The CCP's forces were dispersed into a number of rural Soviets which developed without any close control from a central Party bureaucracy. In 1934 Mao's forces undertook the famous 'Long March' of some 3,000 miles from Kiangsi to Yenan. In 1935 at the Tsunyi Conference Mao became Chairman of the Politburo of the CCP. He insisted on the specifically Chinese character of the revolution—an insistence given formal expression during the 'rectification campaign' of 1942–4. In September, 1949, Mao proclaimed the People's Republic of China after the defeat of Chiang Kai-shek's Nationalists. In 1959 he resigned as Chairman of the Republic, though retaining Party posts. After the Great Leap Forward programme (1958) and the split with the USSR in the early 1960s, Mao came under criticism—to which the 1966–9 Cultural Revolution was a reply.

Mao Tse-tung died in September, 1976, and the leadership of 900 million Chinese passed, after a brief power struggle, to Chairman Hua Kuo-feng.

At the foot of the
mountain
waved our banners.
Upon its peak
sounded our bugles and
drums.
A myriad foes
were all around us.
But we stood fast
and gave no ground.

Our defence was strong
as a mighty wall.
Our wills united
to form a fortress.
From Huangyangchieh
came the thunder of guns
And the army of our foes
has fled into the night!

MAO TSE-TUNG, Chingkang Mountain, 1928.[1]

In 1949, Maoism appeared to be potentially the most effective of contemporary revolutionary theories. The length of the period of struggle (1927–49) and the continuity of the leadership during all but the earliest years lent an epic character to the Chinese experience. Here, it seemed, was a model of revolution which would ensure success for the poor, the weak and the technologically backward, even against the resources of a relatively modern adversary. Mao's victory was gained against overwhelming odds. Nor was his triumph based on aid from abroad—indeed it overcame external forces ranged against it. It seemed that Mao's comprehensive defeat of the Nationalists confirmed, in the most complete manner possible, the validity of his earlier views. Chiang's Nationalist Armies were demoralized; their collapse was apparently due to the inferior political order which they represented.

So dramatic a presentation of revolutionary strategy led naturally to attempts to generalize from the Chinese experience. Others could see themselves in a similar position and believe that the adoption of a Maoist strategy would lead to a similar victory. In 1965 Lin Piao, then Mao's heir apparent, proclaimed the international character of Mao's precepts:

Comrade Mao Tse-tung's theory of people's war has been proved by the long practice of the Chinese revolution to be invincible. It has not only been valid for China, it is a great contribution to the revolutionary struggle of the oppressed nations throughout the world . . . the Chinese revolution has successfully solved the problem of how to link up the national democratic with the Socialist revolution in the colonial and semi-colonial countries.[2]

Yet those who have attempted to follow the Chinese path have failed. In Malaya (1948–56) the Communists were defeated. Not one of the Maoist-style guerrilla movements in Asia, Africa or South America has been successful. Western admirers of Mao have talked of 'the villages surrounding the towns' in a psychological rather than a physical sense (which latter is anyway clearly irrelevant in Europe and North America)—but their influence on political events has been nil. Attempts to see Maoism in global terms, as the poor nations surrounding the rich, carry little conviction when the only 'backward' nations which can exert a serious influence in world affairs are those which happen to possess a scarce natural resource.

What then went wrong? Why did the Maoist model prove so singularly unsuccessful?

'Maoism' (as distinct from the actual teachings of Mao Tse-tung) was firstly the victim of the ideological requirements of Marxist-Leninist theory. A doctrine in which a basic tenet is that class interests are more important than those of the nation contains the seeds of its own destruction when applied by dogmatic adherents. The division of international society horizontally on class lines leads to the glossing over of ethnic and national differences.

In fact the revolutionary theory, the overall strategy and the military tactics of Mao Tse-tung were highly specific to China. Further, they were specific to a precise stage in Chinese historical development. It was Mao's destiny to unite in his person a number of separate historical tendencies; evolution, not revolution, was his principle characteristic.

Mao Tse-tung was intensely patriotic—culturally, politically, economically. Patriotism required the modernization of a China which had been ruled for half a century by the reactionary Empress Dowager. While, during the same period, Japan had adopted the techniques of the industrial world, China had remained a feudal country with her economy dominated by foreigners. The Boxer Rebellion (1900) was an expression of the disgust and hatred of a people who saw their heritage being destroyed and their pride humbled by aliens. Reform was impossible; only violent change seemed to offer any opportunity for the recovery of a Chinese dignity. Nationalism was thus the driving force of the younger generation at the turn of the century. So vast was the country and so inexperienced the idealistic reformers that, when the old dynasty collapsed, no sufficiently strong central authority could emerge to exercise a new form of control. From 1916 to 1926 China lapsed into 'War Lordism'. In this age of confusion military adventurers competed for foreign support and tried to control Peking in order to lay their hands on the taxes. The nationalism latent in the Chinese people burst out in 1919 when the country's interests were ignored at the Paris Peace Conference. The 'May 4th' movement agitated for a China which was independent and modern. Foreigners, devious and corrupt, were the popular scapegoats. Intellectuals might try to look deeper and work for a scientific and democratic China—but this could only come through harnessing the deeper forces of hatred and despair. Mao shared these emotions; accused, in 1919, of being a radical, he replied:

'What is a radical? He is no more than a patriot who fights for the interests of his country and for liberation from despotic rule.'

Mao's ability to recognize and mould the xenophobia of the Chinese people was crucial to his ultimate success. The political capital of nationalist sentiment could be harnessed to the needs of the Party. If he could characterize his enemies as 'foreign lackeys' they would be destroyed. Success would lie with him who stood for China.

The China of Mao's youth was not only semi-colonial, it was also feudal. This feudalism affected not only property relationships and taxation but also modes of thought. Superstition was rife in all classes. In 1918 the Pesidential election required the prior agreement of a fortune-teller. Dead generals were consulted via séances in the hope that they might compensate for the shortcomings of the ones who were alive. The soldiers of the Governor of Hunan wrote *Te* (to win) and *Sheng* (victory) on their hands before battle. Horoscopes determined the dates of important events.

Underpinning this system was the teaching of Confucianism which inculcated not merely an admirable filial piety but a paternal relationship of duty and obedience throughout society. Whatever its original intentions, the effects of Confucianism were to legitimize maltreatment and corruption. The destruction of the Confucian moral order was deemed necessary by many of Mao's intellectual contemporaries—as one Lu Hsun put it:

If the quintessence of Chinese learning is extraordinarily good, why is it that the present conditions of China are so extraordinarily bad?

It seemed that the furtherance of democracy and science, the twin pillars of the intellectuals' new China, required opposition to Confucianism. What was needed was a change which altered the system and not merely the personalities running it. Yet simply to remove the Confucian order would lead to anarchy. Therefore a new system of relationships consistent both with Chinese and modern requirements was desperately needed. A negative nationalism was not enough. A new order must be created. If such a new order was to permeate China it must be interpreted in terms which the great mass of the Chinese people could understand. The great mass of the Chinese people were peasants. Here then is the second strand in Mao's thought: the creation of a new ethic, not for intellectuals or industrial workers only but for peasants as well.

Mao's distinctive contribution to Marxist–Leninist revolutionary thinking is often seen as his recognition of the potential of the peasantry. Today it seems extraordinary that the ideological requirements imposed by the then arbiters of revolutionary strategy in the Kremlin should have affected nearly everyone but Mao with a kind of tunnel vision. All that could be seen was the example of Russia and the teaching of Marx that the urban proletariat would provide the vanguard of revolution. Yet Chinese history demonstrated that the usual form of protest was the peasant rebellion. Outside China Trotsky had also understood the importance of the peasantry and had urged a policy of agrarian revolt. Lenin too, during his lifetime, had argued, 'We are in favour of a peasant uprising' and had warned of the dangers of 'mixing and merging heterogeneous parties'. However, Lenin had died in 1924 and Stalin was winning the struggle with Trotsky, who was becoming increasingly isolated.

Mao Tse-tung's recognition of the potential of the peasantry was a result as much of his lack of familiarity with urban life in general, and trade unions in particular, as of any sudden theoretical insight. In about June, 1925, he began to work in the unfashionable area of peasant organization. Later, in Canton, he lectured on the problems of the Chinese peasants and on village education. In the eyes of the blinkered ideologues the peasants were disorganized, socially conservative and scattered. Mao saw two other characteristics—they were also the most desperate section of the population and they had demonstrated in revolts in 1926 that they could fight. Alone among the population the peasants had nothing to lose.

In two works, *Analysis of the Classes in Chinese Society* (March, 1926) and the famous *Hunan Report* (of an inspection of the peasant movement in Hunan, January–February, 1927), Mao set out his views on the peasantry. He moved from seeing the peasantry as a 'semi-proletariat' to a more definite position in the *Hunan Report*. In the last section of his report ('14 deeds') Mao talks of the 'poor peasant masses' as having 'risen to fulfil their historic mission . . . to overthrow the rural feudal power'. It is, he says, the poor peasants who have always *fought the hardest*. Mao predicted that imperialists, warlords, corrupt officials and bad gentry would be annihilated by the peasants; Communists could either get in front and lead or be stranded by the tide of events and see the political advantage go to others. The policy of arming the peasants and using them as the basis of the Red Army is foreshadowed in the *Hunan Report*, though not fully worked out in detail until 1936. Thus the adaptation of the peasant rebellion, the traditional Chinese form of protest, to the contemporary situation is a further and crucial part of Mao's doctrine.

This synthesis of Chinese traditions needed to be translated into armed action. Strategically and tactically Mao used methods which were suggested by historical Chinese thinking and practice. These he modified to meet the day-to-day requirements of the China of his time. Experience, bitter and bloody, helped him to break free from the tyranny of revolutionary 'models' and any reliance on the supposed wisdom of the Soviet Union.

Stalin advocated a policy of collaboration with Chiang Kai-shek and the Chinese Nationalists (Kuomintang). The alternative approach of raising a Red Army and arming the workers was supported in Moscow only by Trotsky. In particular Stalin (in 1926) believed that the peasant movement should be given low priority. The result of this policy of collaboration was that the Chinese Communist Party (CCP) was proscribed (13 July, 1927) and then attacked. Forced into a corner by these tactics the CCP launched desperate armed uprisings. In fact the initiative had been lost and the revolt was bloodily suppressed. This, said

Trotsky, the Party owed principally and above all to Comrade Stalin. Chiang Kai-shek, the favourite of Stalin, marched into Shanghai and suppressed the militant workers. Despite these reverses the resolutions of the CCP in Moscow (1928) still reflected a dogmatic acceptance of the relevance of the Russian model of revolution. This attitude flew in the face of the evidence; worker participation in the Party had declined but still the talk was of the progressive qualities of the urban proletariat.

The dimensions of the problem were thus becoming clear; change could only be achieved through force of arms by a Party which, whatever its short-term tactical alliances, always kept its separate identity and internal discipline. What T. E. Lawrence called the 'algebraic factors' of Time, Space and Will would have to be used patiently against an enemy who then appeared stronger and better equipped than the forces of the CCP. There was to be no *coup d'état*, no barricade revolution, no seizing of cities or of Government offices . . . only a slow process of attrition of the enemy's strength and will.

On 5 April, 1929, Mao explained his ideas on guerrilla warfare in a letter to Li Li-san. This contains the essence of Mao's theories which were to be put into practice in the ensuing years. While Li Li-san was arguing for an orthodox Russian-style revolution with the urban proletariat giving the lead Mao was, in contrast, basing his approach on the historic pattern of Chinese peasant warfare. Revolutionary potential was to be found in the peasants as well as in the cities. Mao strategy stemmed as much from the great Chinese theorist of war, Sun Tzu (fourth century BC) as from any Marxist–Leninist dogma. 'Supreme excellence,' asserted Sun Tzu, 'consists in breaking the enemy's will without fighting'; the highest form of generalship is to frustrate the enemy's intentions, the next to prevent the unifying of the enemy's forces, the next to fight pitched battles . . . and the worst to lay siege to fortified cities. Study the circumstances, says Sun Tzu, so that you do not attack an enemy 'whose banners are in perfect order' or who has carefully deployed in a chosen position. To Sun Tzu generalship is the application of a calm intelligence to all aspects of a situation.

Certainly the similarity of Mao's thought in the 5 April letter to that of Sun Tzu is striking. The tactics, writes Mao, must be those of the guerrilla. Guerrillas should be a political weapon, being sent out in small groups like missionaries to rouse the people (what T. E. Lawrence called 'preaching') but coming together for armed action against the enemy. Such an approach required a highly disciplined system of command and control. The human flotsam and jetsam which would compose the raw material of Mao's armies—deserters, prisoners and war-lord soldiers as well as peasants—would need to be trained politically in a new type of democratic military organization. Once highly trained, the guerrillas could be used in a sophisticated manner; like a net such forces could be cast wide or drawn together. If the enemy advances the guerrillas retreat before him—for the aim is not to hold territory but to remain in being and to exhaust the opposition. Should the enemy halt, the guerrillas tire him with pin-prick attacks. When the enemy is fatigued or disperses his forces the guerrillas concentrate in order to gain a local superiority—and then attack. When the enemy retreats, the guerrillas pursue. Like Lenin (and with the anarchic example of the bands of war-lords rampaging through China) Mao was determined that a highly disciplined Red Army must be created. To be classified as 'mere bandits' would be fatal to the strategic purpose of the Red Army—which was a political purpose. By 1930 Mao was emphasizing the importance of organizing safe base areas in which the political purpose could be forged and the Red Guards transformed into a Red Army. Mao called for patience and condemned 'revolutionary impetuosity'; the crucial factors to him were Time and Space in which to arm and train the political Will to win.

It was from such beginnings that the Maoist strategy of People's War was developed.

The prerequisities of this Maoist theory are the mobilization and organization of a population which can sustain, hide and provide manpower for the future Red Army. Guerrilla warfare derives from the masses of the people and is supported by them—it cannot flourish if it alienates their sympathies. Technological superiority must be countered by the organization of a hostile population. In the long term the support of that population must be achieved by a political programme (for example of land reform or resistance to a common external enemy). A parallel hierarchy will be created within a sympathetic population. This will offer an alternative form of government and administration with its own system of law and swift justice. The guerrillas themselves must take a deep interest in the living conditions of the people: 'the wooden bridge over there is too narrow . . . should not repairs be made?' The people must be taught to read for only via the printed word can indoctrination be carried out and maintained.

While those who help the guerrillas will be educated and protected those who do not will be shown no mercy. A Red Army, recruited from such a population, must itself become a political weapon, morally as well as militarily superior to its enemy. As early as 1928 Mao Tse-tung established his three rules of discipline (obey orders, don't steal, hand in what you capture) and eight points of attention (which may be summarized as courtesy and respect to people and property).

The Army thus created must operate within a clearly defined political context, the Party must 'control the gun' for 'war is politics with blood'. In the end it is people, not weapons, which are decisive. Mao is therefore contemptuous of conventional considerations of military glory and prestige; the ability to run away is one of the main characteristics of the guerrilla—and knowing when to, of the leader. Running away enables the guerrilla to regain the initiative and live to fight another day.

In the particular conditions of Mao's China the cities

could be isolated from each other and choked of resources by the guerrillas' control of the villages. Such a policy would render large military operations unnecessary. A concentration of force would be required to gain small tactical victories with the aim of destroying the enemy's forces rather than to occupy towns or strong points. Both 'guerrillaism' (the dispersal of forces into small ineffective packets) and over-concentration in a Red Army must be avoided— good communications and mobility would enable the CCP to have the advantages of both without their drawbacks. Guerrilla forces—an armed people—and a professional Red Army are *both* necessary; two arms of the same man, Mao called them.

Tactically, Mao's ideas are orthodox; surprise, local superiority, harassment, 'human wave' attacks to overcome weaponry and, more unusually, the importance of political indoctrination between battles, both of the soldiery and of the population.

Yet in operation Mao's campaigns looked very like earlier peasant revolutions in Chinese history when similar base areas were used. Ch'en[3] gives six examples from AD 18 to 1864 of peasant rebellions lasting for between seven and sixteen years. Mao himself has been compared to the patriotic military leader and poet Hsin Ch'i-chi (1140–1207). In more recent years Mao has continued to refer to the importance of Chinese historical experience. Speaking to a 'Group Leaders' Forum' of the Military Affairs Committee in 1958 he pointed out that Ts'ao Ts'ao (115–220) knew how to fight wars too; 'China's past', said Chairman Mao, 'has quite a lot to offer' and he concluded by referring to Sun Tzu. At the Chengtu Conference (1958) Mao suggested that there was a danger of the Party forgetting the lessons of Chinese historical experience. When confronted by alternative courses of action the Party should choose those 'which are more suited to Chinese conditions'.[4]

Where then is Mao Tse-tung to be placed as a theorist of revolutionary war? Certainly his dictums have frequently been torn from their political and military contexts. Speeches and letters written for a specific occasion and to meet an urgent practical problem have been raised to the level of eternally valid principles. For twenty-two years Mao was operating in a tense and hyper-sensitive military environment. He hedged his precepts with so many warnings and exceptions as to render them little more than exhortations, but none the less important for that since his statements were weapons to affect his men's minds. The so-called 'Three Stage Theory' of People's War, for example, is usually quoted from a speech *On the Protracted War*, given to a conference (May–June, 1938) which took place against the background of a dangerously declining situation in the struggle against Japan. Mao was thus seeking to re-assure his audience that time was on their side, and that events which seemed depressing were part of a general pattern leading to inevitable victory. It was not a detailed analytical treatise; at best it was a propaganda exercise backed by plausible generalizations, at worst a revolutionary slogan.

Simple general models allegedly derived from Mao—e.g. a 'Two Stage' theory from guerrilla to mobile warfare (against the Nationalists) and a 'Three Stage' approach for the Japanese (defensive mobile warfare, guerrilla warfare to seek Time and Space and then counter-offensive mobile warfare again)[5]—tend to ignore the specific situation in which such doctrines were enunciated. Mao was not operating in a vacuum but reacting to a violent and rapidly changing environment. The effect of Japanese actions, for example, especially the 'kill all, burn all, destroy all' campaign, served to unite the survivors behind those who were the active representatives of nationalism in their area; Mao had to see to it that those representatives were members of the CCP. Japanese use of Nationalist defectors as puppets helped to discredit Chiang. Mao had to inspire fanaticism and maintain political credibility in relation to the Nationalists. He was helped in these aims by the corruption and lack of direction of his rivals who wanted to win, but never clearly understood what for. Thus as the Red Army went on to the offensive in the Civil War the Nationalists simply deserted to them or crumbled away. It was not a victory of weaponry but of morale.

Mao Tse-tung's distinctive contributions lie in his thorough-going applications of Clausewitzian principles to the situation in which he found himself. The Maoist soldier is both political agitator and exemplar of the new order. In strategic practice the principle of unity of political/military effort has had no more skilled proponent. Mao elevated guerrilla warfare from a preliminary or irritant adjunct to 'real war' into an integral and continuing part of the process of 'politics with blood'. He applied the Trotskyist principle of 'parallel hierarchies' to the situation in China and proved its validity in practice.

As a blue-print for revolutionary success Maoism has proved disappointing, but as an inspiration and example it has certainly been infectious. Practical failures are not Mao's fault; overenthuastic adherents have expected too much from mechanical applications of Maoist theory. Mao himself understood the global example of his victory in terms of encouragement and propaganda and not as a recipe for instant revolutionary success. The triumph of the Chinese Revolution, he said, would gladden and inspire, and be of assistance to oppressed peoples.

The Chinese have not been as enthusiastic in the practical export of their revolution as their propaganda might suggest. Where they have intervened their performance has generally not been impressive; there has been, in the words of one expert, 'violent talk and practical non-performance'.[6] The requirements of the Cultural Revolution inside China produced a distortion of Chinese action from 1967 to 1971 but thereafter the pattern became 'national interest' rather than 'revolutionary'. Peking's attitude seemed to be that verbal and low-level support for insurgency might pay off but if they didn't nothing much had been lost. Certainly no 'adventurism' which might endanger the security and well-being of the People's Republic of China has been attempted. The doctrine of People's War has been interpreted to suit Chinese foreign policy requirements. In Burma, Thailand and Vietnam the Chinese have given clear and direct support. A more equivocal policy has been pursued in Malaysia; elsewhere Chinese policy has been calculated on a pragmatic cost-effective basis rather than ideologically. Chinese policy has been more successful in supporting potentially friendly Governments, even of different ideological hue, via aid and advice rather than in undermining them by guerrilla action.

Mao Tse-tung was above all a man of his people. He never went abroad, even when given the opportunity, preferring to improve his understanding of his own country. The essence of his approach is contained in a statement made in 1936, which demonstrates the strength of Maoism and at the same time implicitly warns against generalizing from it:

We are now engaged in a war; our war is a revolutionary war; and our revolutionary war is being waged in this semi-feudal, semi-colonial country of China. Thus we must not only study the laws of war in general, but also the laws of a particular revolutionary war and, moreover, the laws of the even more particular revolutionary war in China.[7]

NOTES

1 Translated Bullock and Ch'en in *Mao and the Chinese Revolution*, OUP, 1965, p 323
2 Quoted Schram and D'Encausse, *Marxism and Asia*, Allen Lane, Penguin, 1969, p 355
3 Ch'en, *Mao and the Chinese Revolution*, op cit, p 224
4 *Mao Tse-tung Unrehearsed*, ed. Schram, Pelican, 1974, pp 96 and 130
5 e.g. McCuen, *The Art of Counter-Revolutionary War*, Faber & Faber, 1966, pp 40 to 41

6 Chalmers Johnson, *Autopsy on People's War*, University of
   California Press, 1973, p 33
7 Quoted Schram, *The Political Thought of Mao Tse-tung*, Pelican,
   1969, p 275

CHAPTER 6

Lawrence

THOMAS EDWARD LAWRENCE was born on 15 August, 1888, at Remadoc, North Wales. He attended Oxford High School and Jesus College and during the course of his studies visited France and Syria. He graduated with First Class Honours in History and his thesis was published many years later as *Crusader Castles* (1936). Deeply interested in archaeology, he was involved in the expedition to Carchemish. In January, 1914, he took part in a military intelligence foray into the Sinai desert. After working with military intelligence in Cairo (from October, 1914) he went, in 1916, to Jidda as liaison officer to Feisal to assist in an Arab uprising against Turkish suzerainty. In 1917 Feisal's forces came under Allenby's command and Lawrence's efforts seemed crowned by the triumphal entry into Damascus. The peace settlement seemed to Lawrence to cheat the Arabs of the gains which they had bought with their blood. His guilt at the betrayal of the Arabs was somewhat alleviated by his allies' becoming the rulers of Iraq and Transjordan, an outcome on which, as Middle East adviser to the Government, he had had some influence. After retiring from public life and serving in the ranks of the Royal Air Force and the Tank Corps, Lawrence eventually tried to settle down at his cottage in Dorset. Shortly afterwards, in May, 1935, he was thrown from his motor-cycle and fatally injured.

'In combination of personality and intellect, of capacity for action and reflection, he surpassed any man I have met.' B. H. LIDDELL HART[1]

T. E. Lawrence helped to lead a revolutionary war which aimed to overthrow Turkish Imperial rule in the name of Arab independence. Being intelligent and sensitive he grasped the importance of the psychological dimension. Free from the constrictions of hidebound military tradition, he used his understanding of the Arab and Turkish minds to organize a campaign which might build the confidence of his men while undermining that of the enemy. Out of his thought and experience he spun a theory of guerrilla warfare so brilliantly expressed that it created a myth in which the quality of his military thought has been all but lost, obscured by the romantic figure, 'Lawrence of Arabia'.

In his time Lawrence was the object of a worship which today would be unthinkable; for example one might take Sir Ronald Storrs, writing of his vigil by the dead hero:

> It was somehow unreal to be watching beside him in these cerements, so strangely resembling the *aba*, the *kuffiya* and the *aqal* of an Arab chief, as he lay in his last littlest room, very grave and strong and noble. Selfish to be alone with this splendour . . .[2]

Storrs and Liddell Hart between them bear witness to both the spiritual and intellectual aspects of Lawrence's thought and attraction, while Churchill called him, 'One of the greatest beings of our time'.

Today, however, heroes are out of fashion; in the West we have none, and should any show signs of heroism we are at pains swiftly to destroy them. Strangely our cynicism ends at our own borders—beyond them, we are convinced, lie great men in profusion. So it is that the mythology of our times contains Mao Tse-tung, Ho Chi Minh and Che Guevera, while the mere proposition of a de Gaulle or a Churchill for inclusion in the pantheon would be greeted with derision. Thus, with Lawrence, this generation has replaced idolatry with an almost total cynicism; since we cannot believe that any man can transcend the sum of his faults we have dismissed the total life and considered only the calculation of peculiarities. For the unreality of 'Lawrence as hero' we have turned to the equally misleading 'masochistic Lawrence', 'homosexual Lawrence' or 'Lawrence the tortured soul'. Recent biographers, being as much the product of their age and social assumptions as they suggest their subject was of his, tend to ignore Lawrence as military thinker and theorist of war. Villars[3] accounts him a brigand, with piratical courage and tactical flair but little strategic sense. Others have seen him as primarily a political agent, a spy who was, in the modern *genre*, unable to 'come in from the cold'.[4] Some consider him merely an outrageous imposter or are unable, like Allenby at his first interview, to decide how much is genuine and how much charlatan.

Yet if we leave others to stumble about in the Freudian gloom and quite simply regard what Lawrence said and did we will discover not only an expert in the practices of guerrilla warfare but one who was ahead of his time in understanding the larger questions of the use of force for the attainment of political ends. General Giap (observed going into a conference with a copy of *Seven Pillars of Wisdom* under his arm), the politicians in the 'thirties who wanted Lawrence to re-organize Home Defence and the soldiers who have followed his injunction to 'read and mark and learn things outside drill manuals and tactical diagrams'— all these have grasped an aspect of his thought that is of enduring importance and contemporary relevance. War was to Lawrence a matter of affecting his enemy's perceptions and through them his will; force was one among a number of ways of achieving the aims of policy and 'effusion of blood' might hamper rather than help in the attainment of those ends.

In 1915 Lawrence had observed the failure of German and Turkish efforts effectively to use the Senussi tribes against the western side of the British positions in Egypt. Teutonic attempts to timetable battles as though they were leading Prussians rather than Arabs inevitably led to chaos.

1 Lenin with The Founders of the St Petersburg Union for the Liberation of the Working Class. L to R: Starkov, Krzhizhanovsky, Malchenko, Lenin, Zaporozhets, Martov, Vaneyev.

2 Trotsky in Red Square, Moscow, 1921.

3 Mao Tse-tung at about the time
   of the Long March.

4   T. E. Lawrence.

5   Vo Nguyen Giap (*left*) with Nguyen Van Tran at the 18th Congress
     of the French Communist Party, 1967.

By concentrating their forces for set-piece battles with European troops the Germans had placed their Arab allies at a crippling physical and psychological disadvantage. Physical because in firepower, equipment and training they were no match for their adversary, psychologically because this was not the Arab way of making war. From the enemy, too, Lawrence learnt the virtues of mobility and surprise, as the German Colonel Kress von Kressenstein brilliantly led his battalions in swift raids against the cumbersome British advance into the Sinai desert (April, 1916). Already, a year previously, Lawrence had observed, 'Turkey, if she is wise, will raid (the Suez Canal) from time to time and annoy the garrison there, which is so huge and lumbersome and creaks so loudly in the joints that you hear them eight hours before they move. So it's quite easy to run down and chuck a bomb at it and run away again without being caught'.[5]

Lawrence's subsequent tactics of hit and run, of emerging from the desert seas on the Turkish left flank and disrupting communications before fading away as mysteriously as he had come, were a result of his appreciation of the weaknesses of both his own Arabs and the enemy Turks. His was the war of the flea—and of the decoy too, as he tempted the Turks to move troops away from the intended thrust in fruitless and frustrating reaction to his provocations. In this role he operated most tellingly towards the end of the Palestine campaign; in September, 1918, his activities induced the German Commander, Liman von Sanders, to reinforce his eastern flank (moving troops from Haifa to Deraa) as Lawrence cut the railway lines around Deraa on the 16th and 17th of the month. At 0430 hours on 19 September Allenby attacked down the coastal plain on the opposite flank.

Yet such exercises, however brilliantly and bravely carried out, do not grant Lawrence any claim to the title of strategist. It was rather in his grasp of the psychological dimension, of the need and the means to affect the enemy's will rather than to attempt to crush it by slaughter, that Lawrence is marked out from his fellows. Those critics who have suggested that he was more political agent than soldier have failed to understand that in a guerrilla war the one logically includes the other; the greater the consciousness of this essential unity, the more effective the commander. In this realization Lawrence was supreme in an age where that unity was little understood—and suspected when it was.

Lawrence saw the guerrilla as attempting to turn the population from its allegiance to the enemy and transfer it to himself. The aim was to destroy the legitimacy of the enemy government not only in the eyes of the subject population but also—and more importantly—in the eyes of the enemy's own population too, and those of its allies and beyond them the neutrals. It was a battle to occupy the enemy's mind, not his territory:

> They would need six hundred thousand men to meet the illwills of all the Arab peoples . . . the Turks were stupid; the Germans behind them dogmatical. They would believe that rebellion was absolute like war, and deal with it on the analogy of war . . . and war upon rebellion was messy and slow, like eating soup with a knife.[6]

Again and most relevantly for modern guerrilla warfare (for General Giap applied these very maxims when he made his war in Vietnam an assault on French and then American public opinion) Lawrence observed:

> We must also arrange the minds of the enemy, so far as we could reach them; then those other minds of the nation supporting us behind the firing line, since more than half the battle passed there in the back; then the minds of the enemy nation awaiting the verdict; and of the neutrals looking on; circle beyond circle.[7]

Lawrence's guerrilla operations indeed produced the very results outlined in the quotation. Civilian traffic on the railways nearly ceased, the engine drivers went on strike and the threat was extended to Aleppo, 'by the mere posting of a notice one night on Damascus Town Hall, that good Arabs would henceforth travel by the Syrian railway at their own risk'. He sought also to reach the mind of his enemy through his own Arab officers, who had served with the Turks; 'by practising modes of approach on the Arabs we could explore the Turks: understand, almost get inside their minds'.

Thus initially the guerrilla need not fear the enemy's greater armament, for his blows are aimed at intangibles— morale, will, stamina—and cannot be achieved merely by killing people. So the guerrilla must also be a thing intangible—a thought, an emotion, an idea armed—'invulnerable without front or back, drifting about like a gas'. The danger to the guerrilla as he sapped his enemy's will lay in a 'moral weakness eating into the body which of itself without traitors from within had no power over the will'.

An examination of Lawrence's campaign from this viewpoint demonstrates the quality of his strategic thinking, even as it shows the contrasting German clumsiness in dealing with the psychological factors.

In the beginning the Turks held sway from Syria to the Yemen by virtue less of their own strength than of the disunity of the opposition to them. Foreign influences which might seek to capitalize on this state of affairs were characterized as the ambition of the infidel to displace what was, for all its cruelties and inefficiencies, an Islamic Power. Thus any rebellion must offer a prospect of plunder and triumph sufficient to overcome suspicions of the Christians and to hold in check endemic tribal rivalries until shared hardships and successes should forge some sense of unity, if not of nationhood. Nor did this political aim run counter to the purpose of Allenby. What might seem militarily desirable in the short-term interest of supporting the British Army would, if it led to a rebuff, disintegrate the fragile cohesion of the Arabs and lead them to revert to their Turkish allegiance or simply to melt away back to their tribal wilderness.

'Victories' in some narrowly military sense which involved heavy loss of life to the Arabs were as disastrous as defeats. Live Turks who had to be fed and supplied were, provided their mobility could be impaired, more of an embarrassment to Liman von Sanders than dead ones. Moreover, too extravagant a supply of loot was as subversive of the Arab cause as were too many casualties—in each case they were likely to desert, to lick their wounds or to share out the booty in their villages.

Politically considered, the Turkish Empire was tottering; the object must therefore be not to tempt it to fall back quickly so that it could concentrate its will and remaining strength in a desperate struggle for existence (hence it was well that the projected Gallipoli-style attack on Alexandretta was shelved); on the contrary its pride and sense of territory must be aroused so that it would extend its substance into a length and density susceptible to surgical incisions which would bleed it to death. In this respect it is interesting to compare Lawrence's approach to that recommended by Clausewitz. The population 'takes fire', says Clausewitz, from the example of the guerrillas; the fire spreads 'as it does in heather, and reaching at last that part of the surface of the soil on which the aggressor is based, *it seizes his lines of communication and preys upon the vital thread by which his existence is supported*'.[8] Germany, for her part, was to be encouraged to believe that perhaps one more infusion of her experts and specialist units might perhaps stiffen the Turkish resolution and lead to a 'victory'.

Specific criticisms of particular actions tend to lose much of their force when viewed in this total political context in which Lawrence was operating. The attack on Akaba was carried out, it has been suggested (Villars), primarily to safeguard Lawrence's position as leader of the Arab Revolt. It has been argued that had the projected attack on Medina, which Lawrence opposed, been successful it would have deprived the Turks of the prestige of holding a Holy City (their last surviving claim upon the Caliphate) and freed the troops investing it to strike at the rear of the Armies facing the British in Sinai. Some urged an Allied landing at Akaba or the seizure of Medain Salih, 200 miles to the north of Medina, so cutting off the Turkish Commander, Fakri Pasha, from his supplies and forcing his surrender. To Lawrence these plans made no sense. They would draw off men and material from the main battle position in Sinai and the demands there, or on the European front, might at any time become pressing and bring about a withdrawal with the job half done. He wanted eventually to raise the Arabs of the north even up to the gates of Damascus—to do this he must have Arab successes which could only be achieved through guerrilla warfare. To tie down troops in a conventional assault—for which in any case the Arabs were not trained—was to repeat the mistake of the Turks and Germans with the Senussi. In such static warfare, defending prepared positions, the Turks were resolute and any success would be so heavily bought with Arab blood as to stifle the rebellion before it was well founded. 'On the defensive (the Turks') eye for ground, his skill in planning and entrenching a position and his stubbornness in holding it made him a really formidable enemy to engage'[9]—as the British were to find to their cost at Gaza in 1917. Once involved in an expedition a British Army would soon be dragging its logistical tail slowly up the coast as it had already dragged it across Sinai—and it would then be the British strength that would be drained instead of the Turkish. Medina must be left alone. Liman von Sanders believed that Lawrence's view was correct and he repeatedly urged the evacuation of Medina. Later events also tended to support Lawrence's view; in 1918 the Arabs tried bravely but unsuccessfully and with heavy loss, to take the Turkish positions around Maan by conventional assault—and that at a time when their confidence and training was higher than it had ever been. Similar reasoning led to Lawrence's reluctance to call for a general uprising in support of the attack on Beersheba at the time of Allenby's arrival and to substitute the Yarmuk bridges expedition which, though bungled in the execution, was undoubtedly a correct compromise between his capabilities and Allenby's needs. Lawrence's consistent opposition to attempts to turn the Arab forces into facsimiles of European Armies received further vindication through the successes achieved by his own bodyguard. The conception of a mobile and well armed force was both politically and tactically shrewd. Through its successes Lawrence at once demonstrated the correctness of his tactical thinking and gained prestige among the Arabs with a correspondingly useful amount of political leverage.

Nor does Lawrence's famous success in his one 'orthodox' battle provide a convincing counter-argument to the correctness of his general refusal to become involved in such affairs. His defence of Tafileh on 26 January, 1918, was a 'textbook' operation—and he was correspondingly cynical about it. The Turks were allowed to advance to a ridge which was dominated by Lawrence's reserve position; there they were pinned down until sufficient horsemen were assembled to take them on one flank, while local tribesmen used their knowledge of the ground to infiltrate the other flank. Once the Turkish flanks were crumpled Lawrence launched his assault. The victory was remarkable less for the tactics involved than for the fact that Lawrence was able to persuade the Arabs to adopt them. Had the Arabs not been defending their own lands and led by Lawrence in that role the affair would probably have had a very different result.

The supreme physical demonstration of the validity of his views was in any case provided by Lawrence's original unceremonious taking of Akaba. From that base he could harass Fakri Pasha's communications and raid north to protect the British right flank or annoy the Turkish left. The loss of Akaba meant that German dreams of a submarine base on the Red Sea were finally shattered. By defending the jagged heights before Akaba Lawrence invited the Turks to expend themselves against naturally fortified positions without risking the Arabs in a conventional assault. A series of small successes would build Arab prestige and rally the dissidents of the north, both tribal and urban, to the banner of revolt. The Hejaz line lay open before him—there he could gain both the small victories and the booty which would excite the Arabs still further to the cause of rebellion.

Thus in Lawrence there occurred—because he was both political agent and, in practice, a field commander—the fusion of the apparent antithesis of political and military thought into that higher unity which was demanded by the conditions in which he was operating. He was, as Liddell Hart remarked, 'a unique combination of reflection and action'. A narrower, if deeper, expertise would not have done, since such 'intelligences confined behind high walls' who 'knew only the paving stones of their prisons' would have been, and were, unable to take the necessarily wider view demanded by a guerrilla war. Some, Sir Reginald Wingate and, latterly, Suleiman Mousa[10] among them, have suggested that the nub of Lawrence's success lay simply in the amount of money he was able to disburse. Lawrence sought always to avoid the 'charnel house'; the thrust of his efforts lay in his 'preaching'—and bribery was part of the 'preaching' process. Lawrence had to create a Will—and to do this he needed Space and Time. Space he had in plenty, but very little Time; to make up this lack he used every means at his disposal—reconnaissance, deception, if need be the sword and, of course, bribery on the grand scale. In 1917 he was given £200,000; in February, 1918, Sheikh Zeid in effect 'lost' £30,000 which had been handed to him to further the rebellion. The attitude which suggests that Lawrence's success was due more to the gold in his saddlebags than to any less material factors springs perhaps from a feeling that offering bribes is a less gentlemanly way of achieving political ends than killing people. Lawrence did not share this view. Years later he wrote to Wavell, 'There is one other thing of which every rebellion is mortally afraid—treachery. If . . . the money had been put into buying the few venial men always to be found in a big movement, then they would have crippled us . . . one well-informed traitor will stop a national rising.'[11] On balance Lawrence's expenditure saved lives—both through the men it bought and the men it prevented the Turks from buying. Lawrence also knew when, where and whom to bribe; he had a great capacity for intrigue and the dramatic skill to make even corruption into an art.

In the end most of the criticisms of Lawrence are founded on a view of 'war' as a specialist and separate activity, properly only the concern of 'soldiers'. To Lawrence, on the other hand, war was a total activity involving the use of violence combined with deception, espionage, corruption, propaganda and promises designed to destroy the enemy's will to continue. Within that conception 'guerrilla warfare' was a technique particularly appropriate to the weak who, unable frontally to assault the enemy's strength, must undermine it little by little. It is in this respect that Lawrence's views are of contemporary relevance.

People in Western Europe—and more especially in Britain —have been accustomed to possessing military strength and technological proficiency; as our economy declines, however, and the cost of military equipment rises, we shall become progressively weaker relative to the United States and the Soviet Union, and perhaps eventually other countries too. We shall have neither the numbers nor the technology. This deficiency can only be repaired by a greater attention to Lawrence's 'psychological dimension'. Hitherto we have studied guerrilla warfare primarily in order to defeat it; in our new comparative weakness we shall have to study it yet more intensively so that we can utilise it in order to offer a potential aggressor a prospect of total opposition. In such a situation we must not 'let the metaphysical weapon rust unused' by adopting a narrowly military approach to our defence problems. The requirement will be, even more than in Lawrence's time, 'understanding, hard study, brain work and concentration'. Tomorrow's generals will have to get yet closer to the perfection of knowing 'everything in heaven and earth'.[12]

 xxx

This chapter is based, by permission, on an article which first appeared in *The Army Quarterly and Defence Journal*, vol 106, no 1, January, 1976.

NOTES

1 Liddell Hart, B. H., *Memoirs*, Vol I, Cassell, 1965, p 356
2 Storrs, Sir Ronald, *Orientations*, Nicholson & Watson, 1939, p 471
3 Villars, J. B., *T. E. Lawrence*, Sidgwick & Jackson, 1958
4 See Knightley & Simpson, *The Secret Lives of Lawrence of Arabia*, Nelson, 1969
5 Letter, 20 April, 1915, quoted Villars op cit, p 78
6 Lawrence, T. E., *Seven Pillars of Wisdom*, 1939, ed, p 108; elsewhere Lawrence likens rebellion to 'a National Strike'
7 Lawrence, op cit, p 201
8 Clausewitz, *On War*, ed Maude, Routledge & Kegan Paul, 1949, p 345
9 Wavell, A. P., *The Palestine Campaign*, 3rd edn, 1931, p 21
10 Mousa, Suleiman, *T. E. Lawrence: An Arab View*, Oxford, 1966
11 Lawrence—letter to Colonel A. P. Wavell, 21 May, 1923
12 See Lawrence's letter to B. H. Liddell Hart, 26 June, 1933, from which the quotations in the last paragraph are taken

CHAPTER 7

Giap

VO NGUYEN GIAP was born in 1912 at Quang Binh. He was educated at the French Lycée in Hué and at the University of Hanoi where he gained a doctorate in law. In about 1930 Giap became a member of the Indo-Chinese Communist Party. After teaching history at Thong Lang School, Hanoi, he joined Ho Chi Minh in China in 1940. From then on he was involved in training guerrillas for action against the Japanese and their French collaborators. Giap became Minister of the Interior in 1945 and later Minister of Defence and C in C of the North Vietnamese Army. Since the Viet Minh triumph at Dien Bien Phu in 1954, Giap has served as a vice premier of North Vietnam and a member of the Politburo of the Lao Dong (Workers' Party). After a period of partial eclipse in the early 1960s, he once more returned to influence and directed the North Vietnamese Army strategy against the South Vietnamese and American forces which ultimately led to US withdrawal and the unification of Vietnam. At the time of writing he is a deputy prime minister and Minister of Defence in an administration headed by Pham Van Dong.

'If the defenders don't win, they lose; if the guerrillas don't lose, they win.'

'The enemy will be caught in a dilemma; he has to drag out the war in order to win it and does not possess, on the other hand, the psychological and political means to fight a long-drawn-out war.' VO NGUYEN GIAP

All generals, whether they like it or not, are political generals; if what they do is not politics, then it is butchery. In peace their existence and potential for violence either supports or threatens the political order of their countries. Some generals realize these things, some resent them, some rebel against them, some pretend not to notice . . . but those who willingly accept their political character and see into their enemy's minds in the light of it, these are the few who come closest to genius. It is because General Giap judged his actions, his opponent's gains and his own losses against the single standard of political effectiveness, allowing no irrelevant considerations of prestige or sentiment to interfere with the attainment of the political objective that he must be placed among the few great commanders of the twentieth century.

Vo Nguyen Giap was born in 1912. Vietnamese National-ism, though it had resulted in popular risings between 1885 and 1888 (in which Giap's father had been involved) was relatively dormant during Giap's early years. In the early 1920s, however, the desire for Vietnamese independence grew and found expression in a number of political move-ments. Revolutionary and moderate groups competed for the allegiance of Vietnamese patriots. The mental frame of reference of many Vietnamese was as much European as Asiatic. Feelings towards the French were therefore mixed. Admiration for French culture could have been turned to political advantage but the rate of assimilation of Vietnamese into French society was painfully slow. It is not therefore surprising that another European tradition, that of self-determination, should have proved attractive to some young Vietnamese.

Ho Chi Minh was at this time (1925) one of the leaders of *The Revolutionary League of the Youth of Vietnam*. The example of the 1917 Russian Revolution fired Ho with an admiration of Lenin, 'because he was a great patriot who liberated his compatriots'. Rivalry between Stalinist and Trotskyist factions constantly weakened the Communist movement in Vietnam, even after Ho had achieved at least a paper unity in 1931 when he set up the Indo-China Communist Party. Lack of numbers and organization prevented any resort to armed action at that time. This was not due to any lack of theoretical understanding. Ho Chi Minh had studied in Moscow and had contributed to a work on armed insurrection produced by the Communist International (Comintern). Should any further evidence of the impracticality of armed action at that time have been required, the crushing of a rebellion mounted by the rival Nationalist Party in February, 1930, certainly provided it.

Giap was active in student politics and was ultimately sent to prison for three years. Released after only four months, he dedicated his energies for the next eight years primarily to study. After gaining his baccaulaureate at Hué, Giap proceed to a law degree and, in 1938, to post-graduate study. He then married the daughter of a professor and settled down as a teacher of history in Hanoi.

In 1939, at the age of twenty-seven, Giap was one of the intellectual leaders of Communism in Vietnam. He was a teacher, intelligent, informed—but he could not, in Communist terms, be described as a militant. His practical military knowledge and experience was nil.

Politically, however, the situation was promising for the Communists. Only they accepted that ultimately violence against the French would be inevitable. A salutary lesson to all Vietnamese had been delivered by the French when a march of peasants had been attacked by aircraft. This bombing was as useful to Ho and the Communists as the shooting of peasants by Tsarist soldiers in 1905 had been to Lenin. Since confrontation was in any case going to occur there was little point in compromise; the Communist political programme was therefore sweeping and radical. Revolutionary solutions to the plight of the poor were offered both as an appeal to the people and as a challenge to the colonial administration. Others, who sought some arrangement with the French, would in the end be labelled as 'collaborators with the imperial power'.

War, as the Japanese swept into China and, in Malaya, proved that the colonial colossus had feet of clay, presented a great opportunity to revolutionaries throughout Asia. Vaunted European technological and military expertise was shown to be vulnerable to the attacks of dedicated and disciplined local forces.

The Communists naturally hoped to be able to exploit this situation and, in May, 1940, Giap left Vietnam in order to join Ho Chi Minh in Yunnan where they could look for support from the Chinese Communist Party—or from their rivals, Chiang Kai-shek's Nationalists. The Nationalist Kuomintang hoped to use Ho's organization to gather intelligence on the situation in Vietnam. Giap left his wife and sister behind in Vietnam; both were to die at the hands of the French.

The Japanese invaded Vietnam late in 1940. The French authorities were sympathetic to the Vichy régime in France and so were allowed some autonomy by the invaders. In Cochin China and Tonkin there were Communist-led uprisings which were suppressed by the French and their local Vietnamese followers. Fugitives from these revolts became Giap's first recruits in southern China as he turned his attention to military affairs. At the end of 1941 he had about one hundred recruits.

Those who cling to a belief in military mystique and ritual in the formation of military leadership might well ponder the position of Giap in 1940. He had no military experience or training. His knowledge of war was purely academic. He nevertheless had the advantage of approaching the problems of his new role with a mind uncluttered by the institutional wisdom of traditional military establishments.

In weaponry, numbers and training Giap's group was weak. The positive elements in the situation from his point of view were the chaos of wartime conditions, the unpopularity of the Japanese and French and the support to be gained from China. Politically it was necessary to demonstrate national solidarity. Ho was not slow to use 'united front' tactics and, in May, 1941, he set up the *Independence League*. Profiting from Mao's experience, however, Ho was careful to keep Communist organization and direction separate and under his control.

From the beginning Giap, for his part, carefully co-ordinated his military preparations with the political situation. Indeed there was in his mind no distinction between the two. He had a single political function which could be put into operation in many ways, one of which involved the use of arms. He began to run courses on guerrilla tactics. His aim was to make not war, but propaganda. Armed teams, infiltrated into the south, preached the message of national independence. Goaded into action, the French tried to coerce the population into obedience by arrest and imprisonment. Giap's terrorism, however, proved more effective against collaborators than was French terrorism against revolutionaries. For Giap's men could slip across the border out of harm's way. The collaborators had nowhere to hide.

Space was on Giap's side, as was Time. Throughout Indo-China cells were established against the day of reckoning. Small groups able quickly to disperse offered provocation but no sufficiently concentrated target against which an enemy could use the weapons of mass destruction. Since only the Communist Viet Minh seemed to be fighting and generally the local activists for national unity were their supporters, they gradually came to be respected. Nationalists, actual or potential, felt that only the Viet Minh were visibly dedicated to 'independence or death'. National unity gradually came to mean Communist unity, self-determination to mean Communist revolution. 'I was born,' said Ho Chi Minh, 'at a time when my country was already a slave State. From the days of my youth I have fought to free it. That is my one merit.' From this time on more and more people came to believe in the truth of such a boast.

By 1944, Giap was ready for the inception of large-scale guerrilla warfare in order to seize the initiative from the

Japanese as they withdrew. The first unit of the National Liberation Army was formed. This unit attacked French outposts to provide Ho Chi Minh with some useful propaganda. Ho had himself outlined the functions of such a unit in an instruction of December, 1944:

The Vietnam Propaganda Unit for National Liberation shows by its name that greater importance should be attached to the political than to the military side.

This propaganda unit was to be the embryo of the Liberation Army.

By about June, 1945, Giap's Army was several thousand strong, yet his military experience still did not extend beyond the equivalent of a battalion command. Nevertheless he knew his men, the country, the enemy and his aim. Politically he possessed an experience as vast as his strictly military knowledge was limited. Since what he was about to undertake was not a traditional war but 'politics with blood' he was in fact admirably suited to his task.

In June, 1945, a Japanese *coup* removed the colonial administration. French prestige was shattered. Ho and the Viet Minh moved swiftly to fill the vacuum between the later Japanese defeat and the arrival of the Allied troops. In this period the Viet Minh founded their claim to be the legitimate Government of Vietnam. National integrity rested in the hands of Ho Chi Minh. The returning French must be boycotted while others—Americans, British and the watching world—were to be influenced by references to George Washington and the Declaration of Independence. Once Ho could claim to represent an existing Government then any who afterwards opposed him could be branded as traitors or imperialists.

As the confrontation with the French developed, Giap came to enjoy one great advantage; integrated with the political direction of the struggle, he could act instinctively without feeling constrained by some separate and unsympathetic Government. His French enemy, on the other hand, suffered from a distant and constantly changing political interference. Party politics in France might lead to prevarication or the execution of a sudden volte-face in order to buy votes at home with the blood of a colonial Army.

Giap could also be ruthless. During 1946 he carried out a purge of his political opponents in order to remove any rival organization or propaganda apparatus. No potential Government, alternative to that of the Viet-Minh, must be left for the French to patronise. Terrorist operations were also mounted against the French, mainly in Saigon. The tactic of denunciation to the authorities of units or individuals failing to toe the Party line was also used (just as Ho had betrayed one of his rivals, Pham Boi Chau, in the 1920s). Towards the people, however, Giap adopted a different approach derived from Maoist principles. The uncommitted multitude must be won over by the discipline and courtesy of the guerrillas. Giap insisted that his men must respect and help the people, thus winning their trust and affection. Giap's book, *The War of Liberation and the Popular Army* (1950), emphasized the importance of propaganda, tactical understanding down to junior level and the need for all ranks to possess the stamina and patience to fight a protracted war.

In *People's War, People's Army*, Giap formulated the role of the first, guerrilla, stage of revolutionary war in terms which are reminiscent of Lawrence and Clausewitz.

'The most appropriate guiding principle for activities,' wrote Giap, 'was armed propaganda . . .' (the guerrillas) 'had to operate in strict secrecy with central points for propaganda activity and for dealing with traitors. Their military attacks were strictly secret and carried out with rapidity. *Their movements had to be phantom-like.*'[1]

Adept at guerrilla warfare, Giap received a setback when he came down from the hills and went on to a more conventional offensive. By fighting on terrain where it was

86

6 Che Guevara at the International Social and Economic Conference, Punta del Este, Uruguay, August, 1961.

7 Kim Il Sung (*right*) greets Prince Sihanouk at Pyongyang, June, 1970.

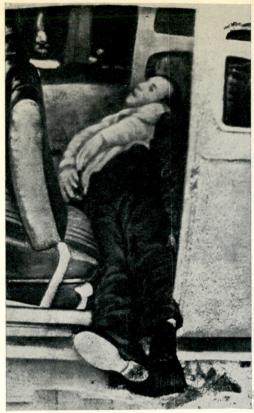

8 The body of Carlos Marighela, Sao Paulo, November, 1969.

9 George Grivas is carried by his supporters through Larissa, Northern Greece, November, 1960.

possible to deploy superior French firepower and aerial strength, Giap handed the initiative to the brilliant newly-arrived French commander, General de Lattre. Not that Giap himself was all that badly equipped; it has been estimated that his troops had some 35,000 rifles, 200 mortars and even a few ex-Japanese tanks.

Good generals know when to run away and Giap soon reverted to a less direct approach. His offensive, however regarded militarily (he had suffered 20,000 casualties), had not been a total political loss. Ho Chi Minh needed such demonstrations of dedication and sacrifice to maintain his prestige. Only thus could he impress the Vietnamese people, especially in the south, with his ability to confront the French militarily.

Once Giap had re-adopted the indirect approach, the French were unable to follow up their apparent victory. However impressively troops might sweep through an area, the guerrillas would spring up in their wake once more. Show the flag by dispersing forces and the guerrillas would achieve a local superiority in order to destroy an outpost or ambush a convoy. Concentrate forces for a saturation operation and the guerrillas would refuse combat and run away.

Giap's decision to cut his losses after the failure of his first offensive was a difficult one. A general imbued with traditional ideas of glorious defiance and 'denying ground to the enemy' might have been annihilated. To die heroically is in fact a poor alternative to temporary humiliation, respite and counter-attack.

Dien Bien Phu was Giap's counter-attack. In that one action deception, concentration and assault were all united with the most important characteristic of all . . . political timing. Maximum publicity and world-wide impact were guaranteed by the Geneva negotiations going on at the time. Navarre, the French commander, was also seeking victory for *his* negotiators. Heroism and self-sacrifice—by anti-Communist Vietnamese as well as by the French—were not enough. Throughout the war the constant reiteration of French casualties and achievements did little for the morale of their Vietnamese allies. Of 1,800 volunteers who parachuted into the beleaguered fortress of Dien Bien Phu about 800 were in fact Vietnamese.

Only one French tactic, cost-effective and potentially decisive in such situations, ever seriously threatened Giap. The use of indigenous troops to strike at Giap's bases and supply routes hindered the Viet Minh effort. Only an immense porterage operation overcame Giap's logistical problems. A greater investment in irregular forces would certainly have at least delayed Giap's triumph. Any successes achieved by indigenous forces would, properly exploited, have represented a considerable political bonus to the colonial Government. However, the lack of any political philosophy behind the deployment of local irregulars detracted from their effectiveness; *they* were brave soldiers, *Giap* commanded a 'doctrine armed'. The French were always worse off than the British in Malaya who at least had an alternative Government, with a distinct ethnic base, to that offered by the insurgents.

With the ending of the First Indo-China War Giap had achieved half of the political aim. There remained the unification of Vietnam. First the North had be moulded to the will of the Party. Crude methods, generalized from the Chinese experience, crushed 'landlordism' but involved great cruelties and the deaths of thousands of innocent victims.

The Second Indo-China War, against the United States of America and its South Vietnamese ally, was also in two major aspects a revolutionary war. In the first place it was defined by the North as a necessary continuation of the struggle for freedom from foreign domination. The French effort by 1954 had in any case been 80 per cent subsidized by the United States. It was the fight of the Vietnamese people, of the nation. That this 'nation' contained many different ethnic and linguistic groups, further sub-divided by religion and culuture, was irrelevant. The people and the

People's Army lay at the heart of the revolution. As the struggle continued, so would the nation triumph over its enemies and, where the nation was unknown, it would be created in the heat of the struggle.

Further, it was for those native to the South a revolutionary war in concept and tactics. For them their 'base area' was the North and the process of infiltration and guerrilla warfare similar to that previously used by Giap from the border areas with China. The Americans were their French and, as with the creaking democracy of France, the key was held not by soldiers in the jungles but by politicians in distant capitals. Behind the politicians, mourning their young dead as had the French in the 1940s and '50s, were the people: mothers, fathers, brothers and sisters. Around the stage stood the neutrals. All were vulnerable to the propaganda of the word and of the image. Decisive moments of drama might be turned to the insurgents' advantage. Military defeats meant less in terms of their outcome than through the impact of their dead and wounded on public opinion in the enemy country.

It was in the adaptation of Maoist doctrine to his own situation and, in particular, in the internationalization of the war so that the whole world became part of the battleground that Giap added a new dimension to the theory of revolutionary war.

What Giap was seeking to do was to exploit his American enemy's conscience and value system. In the interim period after the Geneva Conference the Communists confidently awaited the collapse of the Diem Government in the South. The local Communists lay low. With the relative success of the Diem régime, at least while it was backed by the United States, a re-appraisal of Communist policy was necessary. In mid-1959 the decision was taken in Hanoi to go over to revolutionary guerrilla war in the South. This war was to be backed by a complicated and interlocking series of organizations which together would constitute a counter-State. By 1962 some 300,000 people belonged to these organizations. To propaganda and persuasion was added the intimidation of terror as community leaders were assassinated. Diem's Government, by no means the most ineffective of the series of régimes that the unhappy country of South Vietnam was to enjoy, found itself confronted by an opponent adept at every aspect of propaganda. Militant Buddhists protested at alleged Catholic oppression and burned themselves to death before the cameras of the world's Press. 'Struggle incidents' were organized with theatrical precision. Yet despite all these revolutionary pressures the 'general uprising' foreseen by Giap's rival ideologue, Truong Chinh, failed to materialize.

Truong has been regarded by some commentators as 'a much more important theoretician than Giap'.[2] Politically Truong Chinh was a master practitioner of 'united front' tactics: nationalism was to be used to bind the people together, but the bonds were to be controlled by the Communists. Neither the landlord class nor the French were excluded from such a united front.

Working from 'the invaluable experience of history' Truong argued that the insurgents' best strategist was Time. Time to indoctrinate the peasant guerrilla, to make propaganda among the troops opposing the revolution and time to influence opinion in the opposing country. To operate such a strategy required exact intelligence, not just of the enemy Army but of the views and reactions of his people. Sympathizers in France and the USA were ready to give that intelligence.

Truong places much reliance in his theory on an almost mystical concept of the 'power of the people'. At some point, he suggests, the spiralling pressures of terror and counter-terror will result in an explosion of popular rage and revolutionary ardour which will sweep the Government aside in a general uprising (*Khoi Nghia*).[3] The seizure of power from the Japanese and the setting up of an administration in under three weeks during the August Revolution appeared to vindicate his view.

Similarly Truong's conception of guerrilla warfare is based on the involvement of the entire people: guerrilla warfare must be the tactic of the people as a whole, not of the army alone. When writing on tactics Truong seems more at home when discussing guerrilla warfare in its earlier stages; he recommends in particular the use of disguised professional units, integrated with the civilian population. Even during its later stages revolutionary war, in the Truong style, is deliberately disorderly with regulars, guerrillas, civilian militias and people all acting against the Government; there are no 'battle fronts', the revolutionaries encircle and suffocate the enemy, physically and psychologically.

It was in keeping with these earlier views and experiences when, in 1963, Truong Chinh preferred to rely on a popular uprising rather than on the North Vietnamese Army. The hoped-for repetition of the August Revolution did not in fact occur.

Giap therefore came back into favour. The United States was by 1964 totally committed in Vietnam. Only a short war would be acceptable to public opinion in the United States. Giap therefore determined to make it a long one. The United States' Government needed victory, but victory was unobtainable. All that could be hoped for was a limited war leading to a negotiated peace favourable to the United States. Democracies have a hard time persuading their peoples to accept the *non*-use of military power and the political subtleties of a limited war. Parents do not understand why their sons should be asked to die so that a Kissinger can obtain a better bargaining position at a 'peace conference'. In such a limited war the democratic, relatively open society which cannot disguise the purposes and costs of the war is at a disadvantage. This will increasingly be the case as time passes and the population becomes cynical about the aims of the conflict and resentful of its costs.

All Giap needed was a 'drawn' war. Politically he could tolerate a stalemate, the United States couldn't; the American public would tire long before the regimented and indoctrinated people of Vietnam. Americans after all had nothing to lose but their pride; in defeat or victory Coca Cola, baseball and breakfast TV would survive.

Giap proceeded to attack south across the so-called 'demilitarized zone' to such effect that considerable South Vietnamese and American forces were tied down in a positional war of attrition. At their backs the Vietcong had greater freedom to use guerrilla tactics.

The famous 'Winter–Spring' offensive of 1967–68, the 'Tet' offensive, had as its objectives the urban middle class of Vietnam and the TV audiences of the world. Giap's timing had a Korean precedent where, in 1952, the Communists launched an offensive on the eve of the American elections. It was, as Denis Warner succinctly put it, Washington's 'psychological Dien Bien Phu'.[4] From then on the protest movement in the USA grew to be an important factor in the situation. The war gradually ceased to be seen as 'America's war' and became instead 'Washington's war' or, worse, the 'President's war'. So the Tet offensive while it could be seen as a tactical victory for the United States was, strategically, a victory for Hanoi.

The final decision to switch almost entirely to psychomilitary operations against the Americans was probably taken in Hanoi in 1969. Washington's answer to the pressures of public opinion was 'Vietnamization' which was something of an insult in itself since it implied that the locals had been doing less than their fair share up to then. Nevertheless it was clear that the South would not fall to the Communists by guerrilla warfare and uprising but by a conventional invasion from the North. Far from relying on the 'people' in some revolutionary sense, Giap was now using the sophisticated weaponry supplied to him by the Soviet Union. The collapse of the South Vietnamese Army (before a North Vietnamese Army which the United States had felt unable to negotiate off the soil of Vietnam) was a result of American withdrawal. The American withdrawal was the result of Giap's strategy of increasing all the costs of the war to the point where it became *politically* impossible for the American Government to continue with it. This had been possible because Giap was committed to the political objective; too many of his American military opponents were apparently attached to some *means* of war—air power, bombers or carriers etc. Moreover Giap's intelligence was more accurate than that available to President Johnson, the cables on the latter's desk tended to be filtered through the selective consciousness of many intermediaries, each of whom had an interest in optimism. Washington's attitude appeared to be a classic case of the type of government misperceptions noted by social psychologists—a diabolical enemy image, a virile and moral self-image leading to selective inattention and military over-confidence.

The Second Indo-China War caught the weakness of the West in a microcosm. The North Vietnamese had no ethical misgivings, no bad conscience. For them there could never —psychologically, politically or practically—be a My Lai massacre, no matter how many village headmen they shot in cold blood. The West on the other hand was, and is, the prisoner of a moral tradition which binds it but not its opponent.

The revolutionary has no doubt: he is Cromwell 'doing the Lord's work', Hitler fulfilling destiny, Lenin destroying the class enemy. What most would call atrocities, massacres, cruelties are perpetrated in any war; in Vietnam they were classified as such only by the West. When carried out by the Vietcong they became exemplary punishments, a necessary part of the destruction of the evil capitalist and colonialist order. 'Psychological judo' one writer has called it[5] and in its grip the West seems helpless. News media, in any situation that can be construed, however remotely, as 'revolutionary', adopt the categories of the insurgents. Giap used the freedoms of democracy to defeat his democratic enemy, and others are engaged today in the same enterprise.

It was not the battle of weapons which the French and

the Americans lost when they were beaten by Giap but the war of words.

NOTES

1   *People's War, People's Army* (italics added); this is very like Clausewitz' description of guerrilla activity as 'never condensing into a solid body' or the 'like a mist, without substance' used by Lawrence
2   Fairbairn, Geoffrey, *Revolutionary Guerrilla Warfare*, Pelican 1974, p 202: Bernard Fall remarked that Truong Chinh fully deserved to be included among those contemporary Communists who have made far-reaching contributions to the revolutionary theory of their own movements (see Truong Chinh, *Primer for Revolt*, Praeger, 1963, xxii)
3   For more detail on the myth of Khoi Nghia, see Pike, Douglas, *Politics of the Vietcong*, MIT Press, 1966
4   In *Atlantic*, December, 1972
5   Fairbairn, op cit, p 262

CHAPTER 8

Kim Il Sung

KIM IL SUNG was born in 1912, the son of a schoolmaster. In 1925 he fled with his parents to Manchuria and six years later joined the Chinese Communist Party. After fighting as a guerrilla against the Japanese he spent most of World War II in the USSR undergoing political and military training with the Red Army. Returning as Russia's nominee, Kim eventually became premier of North Korea in September, 1948. After the Korean War (1950–3) Kim removed his local rivals, principally Pak Hon-yong, during 1955 and 1956. In August, 1956, it was the turn of the pro-Chinese faction, led mainly by Kim Tu-bong, and its adherents were similarly eliminated. Since 1961 Kim has been in complete control and the personality cult has grown to nauseating proportions. He has yet to achieve his greatest ambition of ruling over a united Korea.

'Comrade Kim Il Sung, the great leader of our 40 million Korean people, peerless patriot, national hero, ever-victorious, iron-willed brilliant commander and one of the outstanding leaders of the international communist movement and working class movement.'[1]

Kim Il Sung's contribution to the theory of revolutionary violence is insignificant compared to that of Mao Tse-tung or General Giap. Official North Korean accounts of his deeds and writings appear to be good examples of what one might politely call the 'creative function of Communist historiography'. Kim Il Sung's theories nevertheless warrant attention; in pursuance of them North Korea has trained foreign revolutionaries and assisted them with finance and arms. Propaganda, paid for by the North Korean Government, has spread Kim's ideas all over the world. Kim's Korean missionaries of revolution have intervened actively to support insurgent groups, the best known example being in Sri Lanka.[2]

Korean publicity has projected an image of Kim Il Sung as an ideologically brilliant Marxist-Leninist, a fervent supporter of national liberation movements and a successful exponent of revolutionary guerrilla warfare; the fact that his original takeover of the leadership of North Korea was entirely due to Russian influence is ignored. Kim's campaign has been on occasions literally one of self-advertisement, with full page coverage being purchased in the world's press —*The Times* of London, the *New York Times* and newspapers in Japan, Sweden and France being among those patronized.

During the 1930s Kim certainly fought against the Japanese, and their intelligence reports can be used to correct the adulation contained in the official North Korean version of events. In September, 1933, Kim took part with Chinese units in the 'Tunking attack'; the official North Korean record has a Chinese Brigade Commander deferring to the superior brilliance of the twenty-one-year-old Korean. Subsequently, while Japanese intelligence describes Kim as a political commissar of the 2nd Regiment of the 2nd Division, the myth presents him as leading an entire People's Revolutionary Army.

It is possible, nonetheless, to extract some hard facts about Kim's activities which provide clues as to his real influence and views.

Ideologically Kim defended the specifically Korean content of the struggle during the 1930s and so succeeded in identifying himself with nationalism as well as with Marxist Leninism. This was an important advantage since the appeal of nationalism, economic reform and kinship was considerably more powerful in Korea than the alien creed of Marxism.

Tactically Kim recommended the abandonment of fixed bases in favour of large-scale mobile partisan warfare. In July, 1935, with 300 troops he made what was later described (on the Maoist model) as his 'Long March' northwards, away from increasingly active and successful Japanese counter-insurgency operations.

In 1936, a 'united front'[3] with national and democratic objectives of the usual type was set up; by the end of the year Kim was in the mountains just north of the Yalu, agitating among the local population on behalf of this 'united front'. In command of a few hundred troops (though described as 'a Division'), his brief was probably to watch the Yalu river approaches and report on enemy activity. Despite the fact that contemporary accounts show him as opposed to 'adventurism' (and dedicated instead to recruitment and the expropriation of arms and money), he still launched a risky attack across the river on improvised rafts. The attack served only to alert the Japanese who embarked on a vigorous counter-insurgency campaign, based on strategic hamlets, identity cards, food denial and control of the roads.[4]

Kim's forces were soon reduced to around two hundred, but these few were tough and dedicated. Prudently avoiding battle, he set about preserving, educating and training his small force. After 1941 Kim's group retreated into the USSR; their leader may have visited Vladivostock, Moscow and the Soviet Party School at Khabarovsk for further indoctrination.

Unlike many of his contemporaries in the anti-Japanese struggles of the 1930s, Kim survived to return as a subservient tool of the Russians.[5] To the USSR such a protégé had sufficient revolutionary experience to be presented as a hero, but not so much that he could survive without them.

After the experience of the Korean War, when policy was virtually dictated by the Chinese, Kim succeeded in steering a course between Peking and Moscow. Stalin's death and the fall of Kruschev left Kim as an elder statesman of the Communist world and his attempt to produce a distinctive brand of 'Third World' Communism has made him an attractive figure to some Asian and Latin American revolutionaries. Fringe Left Wing groups in the West have also seen Kim as a possible patron, free from the 'big power Chauvinism' of either Russia or China. Until recently Kim has hoped for yet more revolutionary and national glory by attempting to start a South Korean movement on the lines of the Vietcong, as a prelude to a Giap style campaign for the unification of Korea. Although this strategy receded with the talks between North and South Korea, it re-appeared in 1976 as Kim organized violent incidents against the Americans present in the border area between the two Koreas and put his forces on a war footing.

Two aspects of Kim's thought have implications beyond his own country.

He insists on the duty of Communist governments actively to support revolutionary movements, even if such support runs the risk of war with capitalist countries:

To refuse to support the revolutionary struggles of the working class and the national liberation struggles of the peoples of Asia, Africa and Latin America in order to be on good terms with the imperialists and not to offend them, to oppose the armed struggles of these people on the grounds that it is fraught with the dangers of war— all this is a betrayal of the revolutionary cause and a capitulation to the imperialists.[6]

'Revolutionary violence', said Kim in a broadcast from Pyongyang in 1969, 'is the highest form of struggle for freedom.'

Kim himself considers that his original contribution is to

be found in the principle of *chu che*, self-reliance, which is universally applicable to revolutionary struggle.

The idea of *chu che*, in the words of the *South Korean Revolutionary Party for Unification*, is summed up as:

The original embodiment of Marxism-Leninism in the present era and in the actual conditions of our country . . . the idea of *chu che* represents the Marxism-Leninism of our times, the perfect merit of which has been saliently proved throughout the 40 years or more of severe revolutionary storms . . . It brightly illumines the course to follow for our people as well as for millions of peoples the world over.

What it all means in practice is somewhat vague. Kim's personality cult is comparable only to that previously associated with Stalin. Orthodox Communism is replaced by *Kim Il Sungism*. Unlike Communism, *Kim Il Sungism* can be the basis of a dynasty; there is evidence that the elderly Kim is trying to establish his son and his family as his ideological as well as natural heirs.[7]

Chu che is the ideological manifestation of *Kim Il Sungism*. In terms of making a revolution *chu che* suggests a line independent of power blocs, adapted to local conditions and accepting help (without conditions) from whoever is prepared to give it. Kim's own procedure, unfortunately for the theory, was just the opposite; he was Russia's puppet and destroyed the local 'independent line' leaders in the 1965–6 purges

Now in his mid-sixties Kim still hopes to achieve by subversion or persuasion a unified Communist Korea. He maintains a propaganda offensive against the US presence in South Korea, from time to time provoking violent incidents along the 151-mile-long so-called 'Demilitarized Zone'. Kim continues to maintain a high level of military expenditure, financed by external borrowing which also goes to assist foreign guerrilla movements.[8]

Unlike most of the theorists considered in this book Kim Il Sung has not yet finished with 'revolutionary violence'.

NOTES

1 Preface to vol III of *Kim Il Sung*, a Biography by Baik Bong, Miraisha, Tokyo, 1970
2 The North Koreans supported an abortive uprising in 1971; Korean-trained guerrillas also attempted a revolution in Mexico and Kim aided Black Panther leader Eldridge Cleaver, though to no apparent practical effect
3 The *Fatherland Restoration Front*
4 A similar pattern to that adopted successfully by the British against the Malayan Communist guerrillas over a decade later
5 Much more so than Tito of Yugoslavia, to whom Kim has sometimes erroneously been compared
6 See the standard work on this subject, Scalopino, Robert and Lee Chong-Sik, *Communism in Korea*, 2 volumes, University of California Press, 1973, p 633
7 See on this point Rees, David, *North Korea, Undermining the Truce*, Institute for the Study of Conflict, London, 1972
8 The North Korean Army alone is 360,000 strong and defence expenditure runs in excess of 800 million US dollars per annum

CHAPTER 9

Guevara

ERNESTO GUEVARA, later known as 'Che' ('pal'), was born on 14 June, 1928, in Rosario, Argentina. At the age of nineteen he entered the medical school of the Univerity of Buenos Aires. In 1952 he travelled widely in South America before returning home to graduate in the following year. He then went to Guatemala to work for the Arbenz government, seeking asylum in the Argentine Embassy when that government was overthrown in 1954. After meeting Fidel Castro in Mexico, Che accompanied him on the expedition to Cuba in 1956. On the success of the Cuban revolution, Che was given a number of posts in the government: commander of La Cabana fortress, president of the National Bank, Minister of Industries, but failed to settle down to the routine business of peacetime administration. He became a roving ambassador for the Cuban revolution, addressed the United Nations General Assembly (December, 1964) and unsuccessfully attempted to lead a guerrilla group in Africa. In 1967 he tried again to create a revolution from the guerrilla *foco*, this time in Bolivia. On 8 October he was captured; the next day he was executed.

No revolutionary leader of modern times has been the subject of so much adulation as Ernesto 'Che' Guevara. He was a mythological figure even in his own lifetime. He has been called 'the most brilliant revolutionary of our time' and 'the most complete man of his age'. He has been likened to Lev Bronstein ('the Trotsky of the Cuban Revolution') and to Jesus ('the Christ of our era'). In his death he was a victim of his own legend. His Cuban theory proved useless in Bolivia in 1967 when he tried to begin the continental revolution of which he dreamed. There was little chance after his capture that he would ever face a court. A trial would have been an international sensation, posing enormous political problems for Bolivia and the United States of America, whose advisers had been involved in the operations against Guevara's guerrilla band. Had Guevara been simply a guerrilla leader things might have been different—but he was not, he was the great 'Che', hero of a generation. So he was killed. His theory should have died with him, for not just in Bolivia but all over South America it was found to be, quite simply, wrong. Attempts to adopt the Guevara approach met with disaster in Peru (twice, in 1962 and 1965), in Argentina (1964) and Brazil (1965).

As far as the Cuban Government's export of revolution was concerned, the lesson seemed to have been learned. Guevara himself had sounded out the possibilities of leading the indigenous 'revolutionaries' of Africa and had not been impressed. In Bolivia, not one single local peasant had joined Guevara's group. Cuba's next intervention in Africa was decisive, but it was not revolutionary. Although Fidel Castro asserted that the 1970s were to be the decade of revolution, Cuba tried to accomplish this, not through indigenous guerrilla bands, but through the invasion of Angola. In 1976 conventional Soviet weaponry in the hands of regular Cuban soldiers was used to support one Angolan faction against another. The guerrillas, where they existed at all, were on the other side.

Castro may, in effect, have written off Guevara's theory as inapplicable in the 1970s, but others hadn't. Attempts to create the revolution in the jungle, both militarily and politically, continued.

In the West Guevara's death increased rather than diminished his influence. Romantic notions of revolution, which on the evidence of failure should have been discarded, were reinforced. The high tide of student revolutionary optimism of the late 1960s carried Che's memory further into the realms of fantasy. 'For the rich nations of the earth,' lyricized one writer, 'the dead Che is a terrible and a beautiful enemy.' This same Guevara is estimated by another author to have 'eliminated' proportionately more 'enemies of the Revolution' after Castro's victory than Stalin did during his purges; but the hero, rather than the butcher, has survived.

The essence of Guevara's theory, which he claimed was validated by the experience of the Cuban Revolution from 1956 to 1958, was simple—although to orthodox Communists its implications were dangerously heretical. The theory rested on three principles:

1. The 'forces of the people' can defeat a regular army.
2. One need not wait for conditions to be right for revolution; armed action will itself create those conditions.
3. In the underdeveloped countries of America the basic field of action for armed struggle must be the rural areas.

The first of Guevara's postulates was hardly startling; there is no mystique ataching to a regular army which makes it invincible. However, to suggest that victory could be achieved without equivalent expertise and firepower would be misleading; Guevara himself did not make this mistake. The guerrilla army, he insisted, must learn through actual combat. In the early stages the guerrilla must avoid contact with the superior forces of the enemy; he must rather use his time to learn about the terrain and the population in his area of operations. During this period, too, the guerrilla must perfect his ideological knowledge for this will create the wellsprings of morale and endurance. Once psychologically toughened, the guerrilla fighter, now qualitatively superior to the opposing soldier, can hope to out-think and out-last his enemy. What Guevara sought was armed ideology, a Cromwellian commitment to 'the cause'. His guerrillas would be the revolution embodied—preachers as well as killers, a new style of men as well as technical experts in jungle warfare.

Once the guerrillas had become part of their environment they could proceed to dominate their chosen base area. By achieving local superiority they could ambush army patrols and then concentrate to overwhelm isolated military posts. Soon the guerrillas would have a safe base area whose population would be educated, bribed or terrorized into supporting them. The later use of helicopter-borne counter-guerrilla groups was to make this stage a lot more risky for Guevara's successors than it was to him.

The next military stage is to move over to the offensive against targets outside the base area. Every effort at this time should be made to cut the enemy's lines of communication so that his garrisons cannot support one another effectively against the guerrillas.

Ideologically, Guevara was critical of the Party hacks who ran Left-wing politics in South America. Interminably debating about the right conditions for insurrection had neutered their revolutionary ability. They argued that not until the capitalist development of a country had created a politically conscious proletariat could revolution realistically be contemplated. Che would have none of such defeatism. A few dedicated men, he believed, could bring the Government to battle and expose its class character. This concept was distinct from the teaching of Mao Tse-tung; Che's 'vanguard of the revolution' is neither proletarian nor peasant but based on a small élite of professional revolutionaries whose class background is of secondary importance. These men should have the total control of revolutionary strategy; there was to be no question of some urban-based Party organization issuing orders to a subordinate military wing. The small guerrilla *foco* was the 'Party in embryo'. Political and military activity would fuse into one . . . but the soul of this unity remained in the jungle. To the end of his life Che insisted on this point; even in his last campaign when things were going badly for him he still refused to compromise and rejected any help from the Bolivian Communists if it involved a loss of his own control. Writing in his diary during that disastrous campaign he constantly reiterates the importance of this unity of command ('I underlined the need for unity of command and discipline . . . the military commander would be myself and I would not accept any ambiguities on this'). He remained convinced that, in the words of Fidel Castro, 'the military and political leadership of the guerrilla has to be unified and the struggle can only be led from within the guerrilla and not from comfortable bureaucratic offices in the cities'.[1]

The rural areas would provide a training ground, a secret base and a sympathetic population for the guerrilla band. There is an element of *machismo* in the dedication of the Guevarist guerrilla to the jungle, which seems as much a celebration of virility as of revolutionary strategy. Rural guerrilla activity offered a romantic image when compared to the skulking in alleys and the shot in the back of urban terrorism. Psychologically, said Fabricio Ojeda, a guerrilla of the Venezuelan MIR, the jungle was completely different from the city. The dispute between rural and urban revolutionary theorists was also an argument between generations: Guevara represented youth, a new creation. The Guatemalan guerrilla leader, Cesar Montes, caught the flavour of this contrast when he called the new approach a 'radical vision, young, audacious, dynamic'.

Guevara himself was not so dismissive of urban activity as were some of his disciples. While insisting on the primacy of the rural *foco* directing and leading the struggle, he yet observed:

The importance of suburban struggle has usually been underestimated; it is really very great. A good operation of this type extended over a wide area paralyses almost completely the commercial and industrial life of the sector and places the entire population in a situation of

105

unrest, of anguish, almost of impatience for the development of violent events that will relieve the period of
suspense.[2]

The principles and strategic course of Guevara's model
guerrilla campaign are nonetheless clearly rural. They were
based on the experience of the Cuban Revolution led by
Fidel Castro. Persuasively presented general arguments are
backed by further details on the tactics of the guerrilla.

Expertise in surprise, deception and night operations will
characterize the trained guerrilla. Implacable to traitors, he
shows mercy to captured enemies, understands the local
population and respects its customs. Individually the guerrilla must demonstrate his *moral* superiority to his enemy.
He must teach the peasants while at the same time he learns
from them and tries to understand their point of view. Che
is also careful to underline the importance of propaganda:
guerrilla newspapers and broadcasts must always tell the
truth, even when it is unpalatable.

The seizure of power is not the end of the revolution, but
its beginning. What follows is not so much a politicization
as a process of turning the people into a huge guerrilla
army, inspired by the *foco*. This is the only way in which
counter-revolution or foreign intervention can be restrained.

Che's writings, for all their questionable assumptions,
contain commonsense observations on the details of guerrilla
life.[3] Unfortunately his generalizations were further popu-
larized by Régis Debray. *Revolution in the Revolution*,
Debray's best known work, is not so much an analysis as a
rhapsody. Debray repeats Guevara with philosophical over-
tones and attempts to place him in the historical traditions
of revolution.

Debray's thesis was that the Cuban experience had
demonstrated a way of releasing the pent-up revolutionary
energy in a people. The machinery had to exist, but while
old-style Party hacks stood nervously around, the new
generation of Guevarist revolutionaries would dare to set

things in motion. The small group in the jungle, the *foco*, is described as 'the nucleus which, as it develops, will permit the creation of a national revolutionary front. One creates a front around something extant, not only round a programme of national liberation. It is the "small motor" which sets the "big motor" of the masses in motion and precipitates the formation of a front, as the victories won by the "small motor" increase.'[4]

Since the Cuban Revolution itself became Marxist at a very late stage, Debray is logically forced to suggest that the *foco* need not initially be of that political persuasion:

Fidel Castro says simply that there is no revolution without a vanguard; that this vanguard is not necessarily the Marxist–Leninist Party; and that those who want to make the revolution have the right and duty to constitute themselves a vanguard, independently of those parties.[5]

Debray makes much of the importance of propaganda. Initially he says that the guerrillas will be split into small propaganda teams which will take the message into the mountain areas, going into villages and holding meetings. Later this peaceful propaganda will give way to that of the violent deed since the destruction of army vehicles or executing (in public) a 'police torturer' is more effective as propaganda than talking . . . and any speeches delivered after such actions will be guaranteed a rapt audience.

Debrayism is thus a kind of distillation of Guevara and, because it is once removed from the realities of guerrilla fighting, it contains all the faults of its hero writ large. There is a contempt for mass organization: the Government is not to be out-administered but out-fought. Political programmes are seen as secondary to the business of fighting. The élitist nature of Guevarism is made clear:

By virtue of the social situation in many Latin-American countries (the vanguard role) goes to students and revolutionary intellectuals, who have had to unleash, or rather initiate, the highest forms of class struggle.[6]

It is ironic to note that the first guerrilla bands in Cuba were neither intellectual nor student in composition; on the other hand it is true that Fidel Castro was more middle class than Fulgencio Batista, the previous *caudillo*, who had a genuinely working class background.

As a general theory Debrayism is trebly suspect. Debray is further generalizing the general conclusions of Guevara. Secondly, Debray underestimates the sociological differences between Cuba and Latin America generally; it can be argued persuasively, for example, that Cuba is a Caribbean, rather than a Latin-American, country in its society and traditions.[7] Finally, Debray's theory is based on a selective view of what happened in Cuba, which is supposed to provide an empirical basis for what he has to say. Debray virtually ignored the efforts of Castro's urban supporters. These tied down Batista's troops and his efforts to use a policy of terror affected international opinion. More people died for Castro in the cities than in the countryside. The sacrifice of such men has not received the adulation given to the 'bearded ones' from the hills. The jungle fighter has a better propaganda image. Many of those who worked in the towns were opposed to Castro's subsequent conversion to Marxist–Leninism. Others who were ideologically sympathetic were nevertheless against a totalitarian form of Government. Castro's political and ideological requirements demanded the apotheosis of the guerrilla, not of the urban proletariat.

Nor, unfortunately for Debray, was a Cuban situation likely to occur elsewhere. Bastista's régime was weak. If there were others as weak the example of Cuba was likely to stiffen their sinews. Secondly, there was the now-forgotten consideration that opinion in the United States was largely on Castro's side. Arms supplies to Batista were embargoed and his Army became increasingly ramshackle. The crude tactics of counter-terror adopted by Batista alienated whatever local support he enjoyed; he was in any case a compromise leader agreed on by competing interests for want of a better. His terror policy caused suspects to flee from his assassins into the hills, to become recruits for Castro.

Guevara himself was to discover in Bolivia that his opponent there was no Batista and that the Army, far from 'evaporating' as had Batista's, would send its own 'counter-foco' of US-trained Rangers to hunt him down.

The Guevara/Debray theory of revolution does not correspond to social and political reality. The story of Major Ernesto 'Che' Guevara has many of the characteristics of heroic myth and as such will continue to inspire and mislead succeeding generations. Yet as a practical recipe for insurrection it is woefully inadequate when compared with, say, the doctrine of the Viet Minh.

Of course even those who do not share Guevara's ideology must respect his dedication; it is nonetheless true that the young men who have been fired to action by the Cuban cry of 'Revolution or Death' have invariably found only the latter.

NOTES

1 See *Bolivian Diary*, Cape, London, 1968, pp 14, 29, 36. This approach became increasingly difficult to justify as people continued to desert the countryside for the city.
2 Guevara, *Guerrilla Warfare*, Penguin, 1969, p 43
3 Such as the role of women in the guerrilla band, medical treatment, discipline etc
4 Debray, Régis, *Revolution in the Revolution*, MR Press, 1967, pp 83–84
5 Debray, op cit, p 95
6 Debray, op cit, p 21
7 See Hugh Thomas's contribution to *Obstacles to Social Change in Latin America*, OUP, 1965, p 249

CHAPTER 10

Grivas

GEORGE THEODOROU GRIVAS was born at Trikomo, Cyprus, on 23 May, 1898. After attending the Royal Hellenic Academy, he was commissioned into the Greek Army in 1919 and also attended the École de Guerre in Paris. He saw action against the Turks in 1922 and in 1940–1 he commanded a division in the Albanian campaign. During the German occupation he organized a royalist guerrilla squad 'X' and led it in the uprising of 1944. After the war he tried to convert 'X' into a political party and was an unsuccessful election candidate in 1946 and 1950 (for his own group) and in 1951 (for the Populist Party). From 1955 to 1959, he led the *EOKA* campaign, receiving a hero's welcome in Athens and promotion to General in the Greek Army after the Cyprus Settlement. In 1964 he returned to Cyprus as commander of the Cypriot National Guard, being recalled to Athens after three years. Still dreaming of *enosis* (union with Greece) he went back secretly to Cyprus in August, 1971, and began to lead another guerrilla campaign. He died of a heart attack on 27 January, 1974, and was buried in the grounds of a hideout in Limassol which he used during his *EOKA* days.

Grivas may be taken as the model for separatist theorists in general. The problems he faced and the answers he found were in many respects similar to those of the *Provisional IRA*, the *Basque ETA* and the *FLQ*.[1] Grivas' campaign has been studied by other separatists who see themselves in neo-colonial situations and they have consciously adopted his strategy and tactical approach. In particular the small numbers employed by Grivas encouraged separatists to use similar methods in countries unsuited by terrain or population to large-scale guerrilla warfare.[2]

Separatist movements may or may not be revolutionary in the usual political sense. Frequently their motivation is tribal rather than political. Yet to omit consideration of such movements from a work on revolutionary violence would be a mistake.

In the first place separatist movements are targets for Left-wing infiltration which seeks to turn them in a 'revolutionary' direction. The 'ulterior and sole aim' of the Communists, wrote Grivas, is to make Party capital out of every national movement.[3] Attempts to take over separatist movements will be made not only by Moscow-line Communist Parties but also by various extreme Left movements of Trotskyist or Maoist origin. Contemporary Communist Parties are, however, sometimes inhibited from becoming involved with nationalist terrorist groups because united front tactics with other political parties and working through parliamentary institutions seem to offer a better prospect of success. Separatist groups are also based on the defence of a minority ethnic or religious group within a wider community. Any political movement, such as Communism, which seeks to operate on class lines as distinct from any other particular characteristic (race, religion, language, etc) is thus caught in a contradiction if it supports one section of the proletariat against another. *AKEL*, the Cypriot Communist Party, could not therefore ideologically support *EOKA*, quite apart from the mutual historical hatred between it and Grivas. Similar considerations hamper the Official IRA in Northern Ireland and Communists in Spain in their relations with Basque and Catalan separatists. The KGB does not, of course, have to observe such ideological niceties; clandestine support may be offered to any group (even of a fascist nature, such as the Croat *Ustashe*) which is likely to weaken a State, capitalist or otherwise, in the national interests of the Soviet Union.

Trotskyists and Maoists, being even more desperate for notoriety than orthodox Communists, are prepared to see revolutionary potential in the most unpromising material. Thus both the Basque *ETA* and the *Provisional IRA* have been supported by Trotskyist organizations. Moreover, separatist movements themselves tend to couch their propaganda in revolutionary terminology, partly out of conviction but mainly because they think that this will arouse sympathy for their allegedly 'colonial' situation, both among progressives in their target State and internationally. There is also the prospect that a separatist movement may be captured for the revolution after it has succeeded in taking power.

For over four years from his first landing in Cyprus on 10 November, 1954, General George Grivas sought through a terrorist campaign to bring about *enosis*, union of the island with Greece. Grivas' theory was relatively simple. He would so raise the costs of the British presence in Cyprus that the United Kingdom Government would be forced by the pressure of its own and international public opinion to withdraw. There were a number of factors in his favour.

Many colonial countries, some of them British, were becoming independent at that time and Grivas' campaign seemed to fit in with the trend of events. If he could harness his movement to this political process he might be able to brand a continued British presence as 'imperialism'. Secondly, the British had to rely on a largely National Service Army, whose dead and wounded would have a powerful effect on public opinion in Britain. He could rely on a section of Greek opinion, whose Government would therefore have to give at least propaganda and some material support to *EOKA*. United States' sentiment was particularly important; the Greek community there could supply funds and put pressure on the Government. Grivas' anti-communism was an advantage: *enosis* (union with Greece) would not involve any necessary ideological loss to the West. On the other hand Turkey would not allow her people in Cyprus to be delivered up to the Greeks. The fragile cohesion of NATO's south-eastern flank was thus jeopardized by Grivas' activities.

On the island the racial and religious divide between Turkish and Greek Cypriot would guarantee a sense of solidarity amongst Grivas' supporters. Failure to help *EOKA* could be branded as collaboration with the Turks and a betrayal, not only of fellow Greek Cypriots, but of history, culture and religion. The back-up support of most of the population in supplying the guerrillas with information, supplies and hiding places could thus be relied upon. The Greek Orthodox Church in the island under its charismatic leader, Makarios, could offer spiritual (and material) sustenance to Grivas. Although the island was small (140 miles long, 60 wide), the mountainous terrain was favourable to the guerrillas; an army relying largely on road transport for its movement and supplies was vulnerable to ambush. In the towns the support of the people, whether out of belief or fear, made a policy of terrorism feasible.

There were nevertheless some factors seriously unfavourable to Grivas. The Turkish population, then some 20 per cent of the total, was solidly against him and had its own armed organization. The Turkish Government, whose coastline was a mere 40 miles away from Cyprus, could not risk the destruction of its own people in the name of union with its ancient Greek enemy. *Enosis* by insurrection was unacceptable to Turkey and the Greek Government lacked the strength to defend it or to impose *enosis* by invasion. Britain's presence in Cyprus was important to the North Atlantic and Central Treaty Organizations, as the island played the role of an aircraft carrier and listening post in support of these Western alliances. A quick scuttle from the island was not politically possible for the British.

Grivas' theory contained therefore a number of political flaws but it was still partially successful in practice. Tactically the theory derived from Grivas' experience of his

113

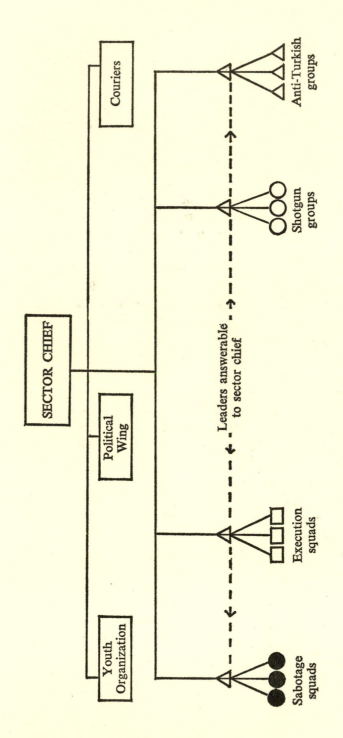

Typical *EOKA* (National Organization of Cyprus Fighters)
command and unit structure in towns

enemies, both the Turkish irregulars of the 1920s and the Communist assassination squads of the 1940s.

Grivas' target was clear: international opinion was to be persuaded that the British were imperialists preventing the self-determination of a subject people. For Grivas 'victory' was impossible; it was also unnecessary. Every action which involved a need for more British manpower meant more conscripts at risk. Random terrorism would tie down large numbers of soldiers simply in protecting other Britons and local inhabitants who did not support Grivas.

In pursuance of his objective Grivas used murder, sabotage and intimidation. 'Executions' of British soldiers and civilians in the towns and ambushes in the countryside were his main tactics. The mountainous areas, together with the support of a significant proportion of the Greek Cypriot population, gave him a secure base.

In his efforts to make the position of the British untenable, Grivas offered a role to all sections of the population; no one was too young, too old or too weak to help. Children could riot, carry messages and, occasionally, guns; youths could graduate from mob violence into the execution and sabotage squads; women could distract soldiers on search operations and sometimes lure them to their deaths. Those who were not able to join the élite killer/sabotage units could organize shotgun groups (OKT) to harass and annoy the security forces. Once fear of terrorism was sufficiently widespread to hamper the routine business of the community, Grivas was well on the way to achieving his strategic aim.

Physical actions were always relative to the overriding psychological objective. In this context Grivas was successful. A sufficient proportion of the population was involved against the British to make a continuation of the political *status quo* impossible. This is not to say that Grivas did not miscalculate: an attempted boycott of British goods failed and murders of women and off-duty soldiers had a mixed impact. They certainly goaded troops into tough measures which could then be presented to the world as brutality. Grivas' policy of provocation via flags and slogans had a similar effect. Troops taking down flags or removing slogans would face opposition from women, youths and children; rough handling meant a propaganda defeat, but so did leaving the flags and slogans where they were.

Makarios was Grivas' most serious miscalculation. Cypriot independence rather than *enosis* was the only outcome acceptable to the United Kingdom, the United States and Turkey. Grivas felt betrayed. His subsequent efforts after the British withdrawal to bring about *enosis* failed. He was then faced with an enemy who was also uninhibited in the use of terror tactics. The second wave of *enosis* (*EOKA 'B'*) was not dealing with 'foreign troops of occupation' but with fellow Cypriots. Since the struggle could not be presented as anti-colonial it stood little chance of international support and risked provoking Turkish intervention. The Grivas tradition has resulted in partition and *de facto* union of part of the island with Turkey. Grivas used terrorism intelligently against the British but seemed so blinded by his own fanaticism that he failed to see that simply removing them was not enough. Greece, although giving propaganda support to Grivas, did not possess the military power to back him in a conflict with Turkey. He could legitimately claim to have altered the course of history, but not in the direction for which he fought and for which over five hundred people died.

Separatists who have followed the Grivas pattern of terrorism have made similar errors. The *Provisional IRA* and the Basque *ETA* have tried to apply the neo-colonial approach to their own situations. Both have over-estimated the impact of assassination on popular opinion,[4] neither enjoys the support of a neighbouring Government and both are faced with professional rather than conscript forces. In general such movements have not been as successful in penetrating the intelligence network of the security forces as was Grivas; he claimed to have known, for example, the conclusions of the British Staff after an anti-guerrilla exercise even before his own campaign got properly under way. The methods of contemporary terrorist movements are considerably more technically sophisticated than those of Grivas, yet he must be regarded as an important influence on them.[5] It was not that his logic and methods were new, but that the international impact of Grivas' activities was so great that even the dullest potential terrorist could not avoid hearing of them.

Tribalism, like racialism, still motivates men to violence. Separatism will produce more future violence than any of the more general 'revolutionary theorists' whose followers will try to exploit it.

NOTES

1 Grivas' writings did not only explain the strategy of guerrilla warfare but gave more specific details as well: his book *Guerilla Warfare*, published in Britain in 1964, contained recipes for explosives and instructions on the manufacture of detonators and bombs (time, electronically detonated and percussion)
2 Grivas' *EOKA* guerillas numbered about 50 in the mountains, 220 in the towns and 750 in the villages, the former two groups being the core of the movement
3 Grivas, *Guerrilla Warfare*, Longmans, 1964, p 2
4 It is interesting to note that Grivas reportedly wanted to carry his campaign of terrorism into the United Kingdom, but that Makarios vetoed this suggestion
5 Grivas made comparatively little use of bombs (for technical rather than sentimental or tactical reasons)

CHAPTER 11

Torres

CAMILO TORRES was born in Bogota, Colombia, on
3 February, 1929. After receiving his early education at
a German School in Bogota, Torres entered a local
seminary and was ordained to the secular priesthood. Sent
to Louvain to continue his studies, he travelled widely in
Europe before returning to Bogota and becoming a
chaplain at the National University. In 1961 he was
removed from the chaplaincy after close involvement with
student politics, subsequently holding posts in the Faculty
of Sociology and the School of Public Administration. He
attempted to unite 'progressive elements' in Colombia
and, in May, 1965, he read the programme of his *Frente
Unido* to a student rally. Torres' views were condemned
by the Colombian Church and, after an interview with
Cardinal Concha, he was returned to lay status (26 June).
Co-ordinating his political campaign with the guerrillas of
the ELN (after meeting their leader in July) Torres
worked for the rest of the year for *Frente Unido*. Upon
the failure of his political initiative (his newspaper
appeared in August and the last issue, after steadily
declining sales, in December) Torres joined the ELN as
an ordinary guerrilla fighter. On 15 February, 1966, he
was killed in Santander province.

En el cielo manda Dios	*God rules in heaven*
y solo en el cielo manda	*And only in heaven does He*
en la tierra do nosotros	*rule*
la gente que es colombiano.	*In this land of ours must rule*
	The Colombian people.[1]

Camilo Torres is important less for his own achievements than for the movement and attitude which he symbolized. An alliance between the traditional mystique of Catholicism and modern revolutionary theory represents a combination of great power. In Latin America, in Ireland and in Spain a revolutionary priest can conjure the spirits of both religions: Christ and Marx, St Patrick and Connolly, Mary and Dolores Ibarra.[2] A film based on the book *The Passover Plot* depicts Jesus as an urban guerrilla who takes over the leadership of the Jewish freedom fighters against Roman domination. In Latin America the banners of Che Guevara are liable to be carried with those of the saints and martyrs of the Catholic Church. Outside Latin America priests have been involved with movements whose motivation is primarily nationalist rather than politically revolutionary. In England, a locally born convert to Catholicism, Patrick Fell, became both a priest and a member of the political wing of the *Provisional IRA*. In 1973 this priest was sent to prison for conspiracy to damage buildings and for helping to organize the Coventry unit of the *Provisional IRA*. In the Basque and Catalan regions of Spain priests have aided separatist movements such as the *ETA*,[3] which has grafted a Left-wing terrorism on to traditional Basque nationalism.

If the extreme Left could harness the power of the Catholic Church (or vice-versa) then there might be a reformation for the Church and a revolution for the people. In such a struggle a man might be assured that in dying for the people he was ensuring his place in heaven.[4] In these circumstances a priest who dies as a guerrilla fighter can be seen as an inspiration both to the faithful and to the godless.

The priest Camilo Torres was shot dead by the Colombian Army on 15 February, 1966. His grave is unknown; dead, as an object of veneration and pilgrimage, Torres might have exercised more influence than he did during his brief career as a revolutionary.

There are certain moral difficulties in priestly involvement in guerrilla warfare, even where the priest himself does not take up arms. The de-personalization of the enemy is a usual and psychologically useful device for motivating and justifying the taking of life. If people can be persuaded to see the forces of law and order as 'a de-humanizing machine' and the police as 'automatons',[5] then such evil puppets will the more readily be destroyed. For the revolutionary priest the uncomfortable truth is that he cannot place human beings in such categories; to him they must remain individuals with immortal souls. Torres and other priests have nevertheless justified their actions (though many would shrink from killing) by talking of the 'violence of the system', thus avoiding the problem of considering the individual policemen, soldiers, government officials and their families and friends. A new theology has grown up: the theology of violence.[6] It is not surprising that priests who have struck revolutionary attitudes have often been students of 'social science'. Sociology in particular has provided a language in which organizations, groups and attitudes can be discussed in mechanical and general terms separately from the individual souls concerned. The Church itself has become a subject for sociological investigation and its opposition to revolutionary violence explained as due, not to any Christian judgment, but to the class structure of the hierarchy involved. The acute shortage of priestly vocations in Latin America has also led to an increase in the numbers of European and North American clerics, some of whom have proved sympathetic to guerrilla movements.[7]

Torres came from the cosmopolitan Latin American administrative class which has produced many guerrillas, both rural and urban, in recent years. Another Carlos, known as Martinez—the so-called 'Jackal'—who masterminded the terrorist raid on the OPEC Conference in Vienna, came from a similar background.[8] Torres and Martinez had a common hero in Jorge Elicier Gaitan, the Colombian populist leader (Martinez' father studied in Colombia during the period of Gaitan's notoriety). Gaitan upset the balance of power in Colombia between the Liberals and Conservatives; his populism split the former Party and enabled a Conservative to gain power. In 1948 during a Foreign Ministers' Conference Gaitan was assassinated in Bogota. In the ensuing period Colombia fell into anarchy as each group tried to eliminate the other through a policy of systematic murder. This sectarian warfare and terror (known in Colombia as *la violenzia*) and the memory of Gaitan provided both a condemnation of what passed for politics and a hope for the future. Later Torres was to make frequent appeals to the memory of Gaitan, who appears to have become a classic example of the martyred rebel who 'lives on in the hearts of the people'.[9]

It is young people like Torres and Martinez, born into the Latin American administrative class, who form the main recruiting base for extremist movements in Latin America. Denied job opportunities, they find a role in fighting against 'imperialism'. The Marxist theory of imperialism has had a considerable impact in Latin America; it sees the USA as systematically draining the economic lifeblood from the sub-continent. This 'vampire complex'[10] puts the blame for low standards of living on a common external enemy, against whom all progressive forces can unite. It is emotionally satisfying too, as it assures the student that the unployment which faces him is the fault of an international conspiracy (just as the German middle classes in the 1920s were willing to blame 'the Jews' for *their* loss of status and wealth). By concentrating almost exclusively on the theory of imperialism students avoid other, philosophical and historical, aspects of Marxism with which they might feel less sympathy. Seeing themselves as the vanguard of the revolution, such young students hope to arouse the class consciousness of the masses. In fact, the workers are to be persuaded to die for a revolution which will put the administrative class permanently into power. In Latin America it is the students who represent the greatest disruptive, and sometimes revolutionary, potential. While an expanding economy can absorb them, in a decaying economy the call to revolutionary violence will meet with a ready response among youths who see a future of unemployment and 'downward social mobility'. So in Brazil Marighela was unable to make any significant impact on the Universities, whereas the *Tupamaros* of Uruguay relied almost exclusively on students and the administrative class. Born into this class, Camilo Torres was to be plunged into its problems and the aspirations of its young as a University chaplain.

The attitude of the Catholic Church towards revolutionary violence has been vague and inconsistent. The hierarchy in countries threatened by revolutionary guerrilla movements has generally, though not invariably, supported the Government. Priests on the other hand have often been sympathetic to any movement which might hold out a hope of alleviating the evident social distress of their people. Perhaps the strongest opposition to revolutionary priests has come from militant organizations of Catholic laymen.

The Vatican, faced with these conflicting views, has tried to arrive at some compromise formula, but without much success. Rome wishes to see change but preferably without violence. Since the Vatican will have to deal with any Government which emerges from violence it tends to temper its attitude in proportion to its evaluation of the probability of guerrilla success. The difficulties facing the Church are reflected in the wording of the Papal encyclical *Populorum Progressio* (March, 1967); this sought to strike a balance between the liberal views of Churchmen in the tradition of Pope John and the fears of local hierarchies (and governments). In strong language the Pope attacked the profit motive, racialism and the failure of the rich world adequately to aid the poor. Violence was condemned 'save where there is manifest longstanding tyranny which would do damage to fundamental personal rights and dangerous harm to the common good of the country'. The effect of the *Populorum Progressio* formula is to leave the question entirely open, since the interpretation of the requirements is left to the individual conscience. An Irish Republican priest might argue that all the conditions are met in Northern Ireland; others would as strongly dispute such a conclusion. A priest can no more escape from the conditions of his upbringing than the rest of mankind and these must affect his perceptions of papal pronouncements (however strong his faith in the universal Church and the eternal nature of his vocation).

Camilo Torres was born and brought up in the most violent of Latin American countries—Colombia. From 1948 to the early 1960s Colombia suffered an agony of violence which at times plunged the country into anarchy as various armed groups held sway in different parts of the country. Killing and revenge, terror and counter-terror escalated during *la violenzia* until murder became a way of life. At least half a million lives were lost. This bitter fratricidal warfare prefigured the misery of Lebanon and Ulster. Torres wrote a study of *la violenzia* called *Social Change and Rural Violence in Colombia* which was published in 1963. He knew the risks of political life in Colombia and later, when he became actively involved, he was to fear that he would be assassinated like his hero Gaitan.

Torres' upbringing was middle class, although his mother came from an aristocratic background. He later found it necessary when addressing workers in Colombia to make profuse apologies for his bourgeois background. Torres' mother, previously married to a German businessman, both spoiled and tried to dominate Camilo, who was her youngest child. An examination of Catholic hagiography reveals that in popular accounts of the early years of martyrs and saints the future hero is invariably presented as showing signs of latent sanctity. Torres was no exception. He was wild but felt fellow-feeling for the *chinos*, poor kids of the Bogota alleys. He produced the school newspaper at the German school which he attended and, his biographers proudly report, spilt much ink in 'denouncing his teachers' (an activity regarded as natural for an embryo revolutionary). He tried to run away and join the Dominicans, intellectually the most radical of the Catholic Orders, but his mother intercepted him at the railway station. Subsequently he enrolled in the local seminary for the secular priesthood and later, after saying his first Mass in Bogota Cathedral, went to Louvain to study Sociology, remaining there to work in the Latin American College before returning to the National University at Bogota as lecturer and chaplain. During his time at Louvain Torres travelled extensively, particularly in Eastern Europe.

Torres had developed from priest to sociologist to student chaplain; in the last role he identified strongly with the students and became involved in University politics. Popular with his flock, knowledgeable about the facts of the Colombian social and political situation and equipped with sociological expertise and language in which to express his views, Torres slipped inevitably into the wider field of national politics. Conscious that ideological rivalries and the memory of past bitterness weakened opposition to the Government and that interminable quarrelling over recipes for change merely delayed action, he drew up a general programme for political and social advance. He hoped, naïvely, that all 'progressive forces' in the country would sink their differences and unite in calling for the implementation of his programme.

The conflict between his priestly and revolutionary vocations soon reached crisis point. At some time between December, 1964, when he predicted violence, and mid-1965, when he recommended it, Torres crossed the Rubicon. In June, 1965, he issued a call to revolution:

The ethic is to be violent once and for all in order to destroy the violence which the economic minorities[11] exercise against the people . . . Down with Yankee imperialism. Long live the revolution. Away with the oligarchies. Power for the people until death.[12]

If Torres saw no contradiction in his position, the Church did. On 26 June he was returned to lay status. By July he

124

was meeting the leader of the Marxist–Leninist *Army of National Liberation* and discussing guerrilla strategy with him. It was agreed that while the guerrilla leader concentrated on the armed struggle, Torres would proselytize among students and workers for his united front programme. His efforts were wasted and his sacrifice corrupted by the usual internecine squabblings of the revolutionary Left, in which each sect regards the others as heretical.

Impatient and frustrated, Torres took the final step in October; he joined the guerrillas. Like others of his generation he left the bickering of the cities for the cleaner air of the country: 'I am going to the mountains'.

He lasted just under four months in his new role. Then he was killed. His grave is unknown. The revolutionaries had their martyr.

'He united the scientific conception of revolutionary war,' wrote his commander, 'with a profound Christianity.' There were demonstrations and eulogies; he was 'among the purest, the most noble, the most authentic exponents and martyrs of the new Christianity'. Other priests sought to follow in his footsteps. In Argentina with the Peronist movement, in Bolivia and in Brazil priests have advocated revolution and in some cases worked inside guerrilla movements. In 1970 another priest joined the guerrillas in Colombia, declaring his belief in a 'liberating and revolutionary violence'.

Torres' main contributions lay in analysing the revolutionary potential in his own country and, in a wider context, producing a justification for violence backed by his authority as a priest and scholar and borne out by his following it to the death.

In terms reminiscent of Fanon, Torres speaks of the psychological changes brought about in peasants by being forced in *la violenzia* to organize for their own defence. Their feelings of inferiority, especially towards urban institutions, are overcome as they realize that they can organize themselves and do not need to remain merely passive fodder for organization by others. In the so-called independent

125

republics during *la violenzia* parallel hierarchies grew up, rather through the absence of any government machine than because of any opposition to it. Education was then seen by the peasants as a needed requisite for command in guerrilla groups. The guerrilla force held out a prospect both militarily and politically of social mobility for the peasants.

Torres grew pessimistic about the possibility of peaceful change. He felt that there was no possibility of dialogue between the classes in Colombia. Revolution became a 'Christian imperative' which could not be achieved without 'pressure from the popular classes':

My analyses of Colombian society made me realize that revolution is necessary to feed the hungry, give drink to the thirsty, clothe the naked and procure a life of well-being for the needy majority of our people. I believe that the revolutionary struggle is appropriate for the Christian and the priest . . . I have resolved to join the revolution myself.

These were lofty aims, but how were they to be achieved? Torres' political programme was sweeping: the expropriation of land (including Church property) and the setting up of co-operatives, no new money beyond the real increase in national product and a return to the gold standard, compulsory free education and a severe reduction of the armed forces. He addressed his appeal to every group: messages were written to the peasants (pointing out that 90 per cent of Colombian exports were rural), to students, to women, to political prisoners, to the non-aligned, to the unemployed and to trade unionists. Few of them seemed to pay him much attention. The circulation of his newspaper, *Frente Unido*, fell rapidly. His plan for a great national convention to support the programme of the united front (when representatives of farms, factories, districts and municipalities were to meet, decide on their revolutionary assignments and the tactical steps to achieve them) became less and less practicable. The only course left to him was to go over to armed struggle.

Tactically Torres insisted on the primacy of the rural over the urban approach to guerrilla warfare; it was pointless to take action in the cities if there was no rural organization to maintain the revolutionary momentum. He called (largely in vain) for co-ordination between revolutionary groups and complained of the obstructive tactics of the older Party bureaucrats. The importance of maintaining the propaganda offensive was always uppermost in his mind and he urged, in his letters, the necessity of controlling a printing press.[13] Such matters are the concern of revolutionaries everywhere and Torres was in no way distinctive in emphasizing their importance. There were, however, two areas in which he showed an unusual insight.

He grasped the necessity of having a positive policy towards the military and not merely anathematizing them as tools of the Government. His approach was weakened by his ultimate political strategy which involved the virtual abolition of the armed forces but in the short term he attempted to appeal to military patriotism:

> Military men: the United Front promises to unify the popular class and to organize them to take power. Do not fail to join us on the field of battle where we will strike a fatal blow against this oligarchy that oppress all Colombians, that oppresses you as it oppresses us.

He wonders what motivates the Colombian military to fight against the revolution: it cannot be the pay, which is poor, nor patriotism, because they protect, not the nation, but the twenty-four families which control it. Promotion, he suggests, is on class lines: the top families provide the 'top brass':

> As is obvious, the war budget is not used to pay the Colombian military but to buy the scrap metal the United

States sells us, and to support internal repression in which Colombians kill their own brothers.

Torres was also realistic about the romanticism of student revolutionaries. How many, he asked, were prepared to put into action the fine words which they preached? How concerned were they in understanding the common people?

During the agitational phase of the revolution, the students' efforts have been highly effective . . . In the direct struggle . . . their role has not been crucial . . . A student's nonconformity tends to be either emotional . . . or else purely intellectual. This explains the fact that at the end of his University career, his nonconformity disappears or is, at best, hidden away. The rebellious student no longer exists. He becomes a bourgeois professional who buys the symbols of bourgeois prestige and barters his conscience for a high salary.

Torres failed, a heroic failure perhaps, but a failure nonetheless. His final message from the mountains was a ringing call to armed revolution—'We say, "Until final victory with the watchwords of the Army of National Liberation: not one step back! Liberation or Death!" '

For him it was death and the Colombian people have still not achieved the 'liberation' of which he dreamed.

NOTES

1 The quotations from Camilo Torres in this chapter are taken from *Revolutionary Priest*, the complete writings and messages of Camilo Torres, edited and with an introduction by John Gerassi, Jonathan Cape, London, 1971.
2 *La Pasionaria*, the Communist who inspired the defenders of Madrid during the Spanish Civil War
3 'Freedom for the Homeland'

4 'The Catholic who is not a revolutionary is living in mortal sin,' wrote Camilo Torres

5 As does the writer John Gerassi in his introduction to the works of Camilo Torres, op cit, p 6

6 The phrase is used by Dorothy Day in her preface to *Camilo Torres*, Sheed & Ward, London, 1968, p 13

7 For example, Maryknoll missionaries from the United States become involved with the guerrillas in Guatemala

8 Martinez was the son of a wealthy property-owning lawyer in Venezuela and while still a child travelled all over Latin America and the Caribbean

9 A universal figure, but especially characteristic of Latin America; the Brazilian bandit Lampiao is an outstanding example of the type. Che Guevara and Torres himself may, with the passage of time, come into this category. (See Hobsbawn, E. J., *Bandits*, Pelican, 1972)

10 This view is developed in Halperin, Ernst, 1976, *Terrorism in Latin America*, the Washington Papers, Vol IV, no 33, Beverley Hills and London, Sage Publications

11 Torres' phrase for Colombia's leading families

12 *Revolutionary Priest*, op cit, p 27

13 In letters to the commander of the ARMY OF NATIONAL LIBERATION, July–August, 1965

CHAPTER 12

Marighela

CARLOS MARIGHELA came from Sao Paolo and, after working for many years as a member of the orthodox Brazilian Communist Party, broke with his past in 1968 and established the *Revolutionary Communist Party of Brazil*. During the previous year Marighela had come under the influence of Fidel Castro at the *Organization of Latin American Solidarity* conference in Havana. Marighela began armed activity in 1968 through his *Action for National Liberation*, which concentrated on bank raids and kidnappings in an attempt to use Guevara's *foco* concept in cities. Propaganda successes, as a series of kidnappings led to the freeing of political prisoners, led to the Brazilian Government adopting tough measures. On 4 November, 1969, Marighela was killed by the police.

'The military dictatorship will be liquidated; the North Americans will be thrown out of the country; the people's revolutionary government will be installed; the bureaucratic-military apparatus of the state will be destroyed'; in these words the Brazilian urban guerrilla leader Carlos Marighela broadcast his message early in 1969. On 4 November in the same year Marighela was killed by the police. Today the 'bureaucratic-military apparatus' still exists and the 'people's revolutionary government' is no nearer being installed than it was in 1969. Marighela failed utterly to change the course of history in his own country, yet his influence has certainly been felt elsewhere. After Marighela's death his writings became known in Europe, first in France and then in England. His 'mini-manual of the urban guerrilla' became one of the most-quoted, if not the most read, of Left-wing works. At first sight Marighela's popularity is strange, since he said little that was new and much that was banal. Why, then, did he become so notorious?

In the first place the extreme Left was seeking a martyr who might breathe new life into the Guevarist tradition, tarnished since the death of its hero in Bolivia in 1967. Marighela's death and defeat, therefore, far from invalidating the strategy which had led to them, instead lent an aura of mystique to his memory. Che had failed in the jungle: here in the person of Carlos Marighela was a hero who exemplified a new approach, in which the city streets were the battlefield.

Furthermore, urban terrorism was coincidentally being used by anarchist, revolutionary and separatist groups all over the world. Marighela's theoretical prescriptions were to find a ready market. Socially and politically the switch to the cities seemed to make sense. Urbanization was a global phenomenon. In Latin America the number of cities with a population of a million or more rose between 1940 and 1970 from five to sixteen. Some urban planners have seen the future of Western Europe in terms of massive conurbations, ranging from the metropolis of two million to the megalopolis of one hundred million.[1] Every city has its areas of decay, usually centre city slums in Europe and the United States and fringe shanty towns in Latin America. Such social or ethnic ghettoes are potentially explosive; high unemployment provides the manpower and human misery the reason for creating the revolution. The late 1960s seemed to be producing the very unrest which the revolutionaries had foreseen; in Newark, New Jersey, in July, 1967, the combination of overcrowding, racial tension and high unemployment (11·5 per cent) resulted in some of America's most devastating riots.

Other theorists were also re-considering the city as a

strategic area for violent revolution and not simply as an adjunct to the countryside. 'Today,' wrote the Spanish Abraham Guillen, 'the epicentre of the revolutionary war must be in the great urban zones, where heavy artillery is not as efficient as in the countryside for annihilating guerrillas tied to the land'.[2] The Uruguayan Tupamaros put the matter still more succinctly: 'Where the population is, there resides the revolution.'

There were other reasons for the switch to the urban areas. The cities contained the offices of Government and capitalist enterprises, what Marighela called the 'centres of national decision'. Communications centred on the cities; news agencies were represented, foreign journalists lived and worked close to the media facilities which ensured that the eyes of the world could quickly be focused on any guerilla activity. Incidents which would go unnoticed in the fastnesses of the countryside would quickly gain national and international notoriety in the city.

The increasing sophistication and mobility of government anti-guerrilla forces equipped with helicopters and specifically trained for such missions also played their parts in the choice of the city as the new area of confrontation. Throughout Latin America, and especially in Guatemala and Bolivia, the expertise of special units, often trained by American Green Beret advisers, had not gone unnoticed by embryo terrorists. In the cities it was hoped that the security forces would be inhibited from deploying their superior firepower. Fear of civilian casualties and the close, confused nature of urban fighting would make for greater equality between guerrilla and soldier. Small groups of guerrillas who could be contained in a jungle setting until the climate rotted their bodies and destroyed their morale would live better and do more damage in a city environment.

Technology, more complex and vulnerable by the year, has its nerve centres in the cities. Target, battlefield and stage, the city seemed to be the new theatre for revolutionary drama.

It was not therefore surprising that an active revolutionary who left some theoretical framework for the use of revolutionary violence in an urban setting should have achieved notoriety. Marighela's ideas, helped on their way by European and North American sympathizers in the media, were soon widely known. The 'mini manual' became familiar to the IRA and the Basque ETA, as well as to thousands of students throughout Western Europe. In the course of this popularization Marighela's unsuccessful recipe became further weakened by being misinterpreted and misapplied.

Carlos Marighela took up arms against the Brazilian government comparatively late in life (in his fifties). For many years he had been a faithful Moscow-line Communist work horse. Yet all his devoted work had brought few political rewards, either to him or to the Brazilian people. The example of Cuba seemed to offer another and more direct road to revolution. In 1967 Marighela attended the famous Havana conference of OLAS (the Organization for Latin American Solidarity). Afterwards, in 1968, he helped to found the *Revolutionary Communist Party of Brazil*. Between 1968 and 1969 a number of small guerrilla movements sprang up in Brazil: Marighela's *ALN* (*Action for National Liberation*) was to be the most successful.

ALN's aim was to concentrate on armed activity right from the start. The Government was to be challenged on the streets, while capitalist and foreign institutions were to be bombed, robbed and sabotaged. 'Capitalist lackeys', especially foreigners, were to be kidnapped or assassinated. Thus the underlying tensions in Brazilian society would be exposed and exacerbated.

As in Guevara's revolution, the Party was to be formed out of armed struggle ('action', wrote Marighela, 'creates the vanguard') but, unlike Che's procedure, this action was to be commenced in the city. Marighela substituted the city *foco* for the rural version of Che and Debray, but he did not imagine that urban terrorism could by itself create the revolution.

133

The ALN possessed, through Marighela, a theory of organization and armed action. Organizationally the movement would operate on three fronts.

Guerrillas, working in small 'firing groups' of four or five men, would be responsible for 'revolutionary initiatives'— terrorism, bank raids and, less bloodily, poster and leaflet campaigns. Such groups would be aggressive in their approach, concentrating for specific actions and immediately afterwards dispersing back to the faceless city hordes. These were the professional revolutionaries.

Supporting the professionals would be the second or 'mass' front; this too was seen by Marighela as a combat front but it was concerned mainly with the mobilization of middle class elements, in particular students, for demonstrations, occupations, strikes and the general harassment of the forces of authority, law and order.

Finally there was a logistic support network supplying, financing, housing and hiding the members of the guerrilla front.

Starting with urban terrorism and psychological warfare, the revolution must ultimately also involve the countryside. Once the Security Forces are pinned down by the intensity of the guerrilla campaign within the cities, then their rural comrades will enjoy freedom of action to rouse the countryside against the Government. A demoralized central administration will then be faced by a General Strike and must collapse before the advance of the guerrilla, who will by then represent the only *effective* authority within the State.

Marighela is at pains to emphasize the importance of the rural guerrilla campaign. Since he never got beyond urban terrorism this further, rural, aspect of his approach has often been ignored, 'We have', he wrote, 'diversified the activities of the (revolutionary) war, beginning with urban guerrilla and psychological warfare—instead of with rural guerrilla warfare which would have attracted a concentration of enemy forces'. Despite the urban inception of the war, however, it is the countryside, not the town, which constitutes

134

the crucial theatre of struggle. Marighela insisted that 'the main effort is concentrated in rural guerrilla warfare . . . as a war of movement . . . from the urban front we shall go on to direct armed struggle against the big estates through rural guerrilla warfare.' The city, he writes, is 'the area of complementary struggle and the whole urban struggle must always be seen as tactical . . . the decisive struggle will be in the rural area—the strategic area—and not in the tactical area (i.e. the city).'³

Despite all these *caveats* Marighela's influence has been entirely as a protagonist of urban terrorism. His most well-known work remains the 'mini-manual of the urban guerrilla'. It is in the day-to-day practice of terrorism that Marighela's precepts have been followed, rather than in the wider theoretical aspects of revolutionary warfare.

Marighela's urban guerrilla, armed with a standard modern sub-machine-gun and versed in the techniques of bomb manufacture, sets out to kill 'high- and low-ranking officers of the Security Forces' and to destroy government, industrial and foreign (especially American) property. The guerrilla must seize the initiative and attack first, using his superior knowledge of the city quickly to escape and disperse his forces. Informers must be killed so that the public co-operation so vital to the Security Forces will not be forthcoming: 'let him who will do nothing for the revolution', wrote Marighela, 'at least do nothing against it'.

By forcing the Government, in its panic to track down its enemies, to resort to oppressive acts, the guerrilla transforms the political situation into a military one. Harassed by searches, roadblocks and patrols, the population will be annoyed both by the military activity and by the failure to catch the guerrillas. Confidence in the forces of law and order will evaporate. The 'war of nerves', based on hoax bombs, disinformation and rumour will eventually force people to turn to the guerrilla as a more reliable protector and source of information than the Government.

International pressures applied via foreign news representatives and organizations will embarrass the Government still further. This scenario, as outlined by Marighela, sounds persuasive enough; it suffers, however, from a number of internal contradictions.

While arguing for the importance of popular support, Marighela nowhere explains how this is to be achieved. In particular he fails to demonstrate how the revolutionary is to be distinguished from the bandit, apart from the honesty of his intentions. Indeed at one point Marighela declares how useful it is for revolutionaries to be mistaken for bank robbers because this confuses the police. It is fatal for revolutionaries to be equated with criminals by the public, but this is just what is likely to happen if Marighela's tactics are followed. Terrorist bombs and bullets do not always discriminate between civilians and soldiers; killing the poor is no way to persuade their families to side with the revolution. Nor does Marighela suggest any programme for meeting the Government's standard response to terrorism, which is the holding of elections to enable an expression of the people's opinion of the terrorists. He foresees such a possibility but contents himself with recommending greater efforts to expose what he regards as the sham of such elections. Lacking an alternative and credible political programme to that of the Government, the terrorist can hope to disrupt, perhaps to discredit—but not to appear as a possible alternative Government.

Perhaps the basic military weakness of his theories is the lack of any strategy for infiltrating, dividing and subverting the Armed Forces. Killing soldiers is not likely to persuade their comrades to your side unless the massacre reaches such a scale that they defect out of fear. Every dead soldier or policeman leaves a family to grieve and civilians are thus turned against the guerrillas. Marighela does recommend revolutionaries who are in the Armed Forces to remain and spread the message. If they must desert, he says, let them do it so as to achieve the greatest political impact. Carlos Lamarca, a contemporary of Marighela's, did indeed leave the Army and form his own group, the *Armed Revolutionary Vanguard (VAR)*. Lamarca who preferred rural to urban guerrilla warfare, was killed in 1971—but at least his original defection might have led to a more imaginative approach to the 'forces of repression'. Yet Marighela's theory revolves around 'taking on' the Army and Police in 'shoot outs' and keeping them in a state of 'permanent nervous tension'. In this situation the soldier knows that if the guerrilla wins, the military will be the first to go to the wall. Security Forces thus have the incentives of personal survival as well as 'duty' in their fight against such urban revolutionaries. If the Armed Forces remain opposed to the guerrillas, the latter stand little chance of success. Even if the Government is discredited by the guerrillas' activity, the Armed Forces retain as effective an ability to become an alternative administration as the insurgents. Possessing a chain of communication and command the Armed Forces will be able (and tempted) to take over from a weak Government, thus pre-empting the guerrilla attack projected in Marighela's theory. Unable any longer to play upon a civilian Government's national and international sensitivities, the guerrilla will find himself faced by an implacable military enemy who, already unpopular and not having to face any embarrassing elections, has nothing to lose by 'crushing the revolution'. The defeated urban guerrilla may have the doubtful consolation of believing that he has 'polarized social forces' but this is of little use to the downtrodden masses he allegedly came to liberate. Only if a guerrilla movement can oppose one part of the Armed Forces to another, set soldier against officer or whip up racial/ethnic enmity in these Forces can it hope to succeed in an urban context. Action on the lines recommended by Carlos Marighela, even if largely successful in a destructive sense, is more likely to lead to a military dictatorship than to a 'people's Government'.

The course of Marighela's own revolutionary activity exemplified these theoretical weaknesses. He began successfully enough with brief seizures of radio stations and the broadcasting of revolutionary propaganda. Bank raids (Marighela claimed that it took the Sao Paulo police over a year to realize that urban guerrillas, rather than ordinary criminals, were responsible) and a series of spectacular kidnappings followed.

Initially the Security Forces were hampered by the lack of any central direction; they tended to compete rather than co-operate. The urban population, swollen by migrant workers from the Brazilian interior, posed social and criminal problems which neither the Government nor the Police seemed able to handle. The Universities were crowded (half the population was under twenty years old) and employment prospects, though less disastrous than elsewhere in Latin America, were not good. Abroad a considerable number of Leftist émigrés were ready to make propaganda against the Right-wing Brazilian government. Unable to stem the crime wave and frustrated by the tedious processes of orthodox law enforcement, the police revived their infamous 'death squads' in Rio de Janeiro and Sao Paolo. The guerrilla objectives of provoking the forces of law and order into ever harsher attacks on civilian liberties seemed well on the way to attainment. Should the revolution succeed in Brazil, then the continental and indeed global implications would be shattering. 'As Brazil goes, so goes the rest of South America'—revolution would undoubtedly spread to neighbouring countries. Even a stalemate struggle between government and guerrilla would be exploited as a revolutionary victory by the international Left. Potentially Brazil was a Great Power and represented a political prize of immense importance. It was therefore vital for the forces opposed to Marighela—the Government, business and landowning interests and the United States of America—to defeat the guerrillas comprehensively and quickly. Ideally Brazil might then provide an alternative model to that of Socialist Cuba.

On 4 September, 1969, the guerrillas carried out the first of their spectacular ransom operations; US Ambassador Burke Elbrick was kidnapped in Rio de Janeiro. To secure his release the Brazilian Government was obliged to free fifteen political prisoners, named by the guerrillas, and arrange for them to be flown to Mexico.

Later the Japanese Consul-General was seized and ransomed for the release of five prisoners. West Germany was the next target; her Ambassador, Dr von Hollebon, cost the Brazilian Government forty prisoners, who were flown into exile in Algeria. At the end of 1970 (a year after Marighela's death) Swiss Ambassador Bucher was taken by the guerrillas; the price by then had gone up—seventy prisoners were set free by the authorities.

Impressive as the coups were, they meant little in local political terms. Indeed one expert[4] has claimed that Marighela's exploits had more impact abroad than they did in Brazil. At home Marighela found that Pele and the guru of a Brazilian economic miracle, Professor Neto, each received more publicity than the guerrillas. Football, rather than religion, proved to be the 'opium of the masses' in Brazil.

The authorities, once roused to the political dangers of terrorism, acted ruthlessly in its suppression. Censorship denied the handful of guerrillas the access to the media which represented their only chance of making an impact on the consciousness of the masses. The guerrillas probably never numbered more than 1,000—and this number was effectively lessened by squabbles between Maoist, Guevarist and Trotskyist supporters.

The Security Forces rapidly improved their technical and organizational efficiency. Concerned with political outlook rather than terrorism, the Government national intelligence service was ill-equipped to meet the Marighelist challenge. In 1968 Brazil's security organizations were placed under a central agency (CODI—Coordenacao de Defensa Interna). The Army buckled down to the task of crushing terrorism with relentless determination. Mass arrests were followed by tough interrogation. Thousands were rounded up. There were allegations of torture and brutality. The guerrilla movement was destroyed. Brazilians were eager for riches ('quick economic growth') and passionate for sport, not for sweeping political reforms, still less for a Marxist–Leninist revolution. Marighela's successor, Camara Ferreira, was also killed. The revolutionary groups failed to maintain the momentum of their armed struggle. Politically they were seen to be irrelevant.

Today the abortive revolutionary initiative of the *ALN* is remembered only through the personality and writings of its leader. Marighela's contemporary fame and influence is a tribute to the contacts of his foreign sympathizers. Whatever respect may be due to a man prepared to die for his beliefs, the fact remains that Carlos Marighela's contribution to revolutionary theory and practice was entirely negative. His political analysis was faulty and his recommendations, wrong in his own country, would be, if possible, even more disastrous if applied generally.

It would be sad if the prescriptions of a revolutionary, who no doubt genuinely desired a better life for the poor of his own country, should mislead others into a similarly hopeless course of action.

NOTES

1 See Burton, Anthony, *Urban Terrorism*, Leo Cooper, London, and Free Press of New York, 1975, pp 6–7 and 240
2 Quoted Hodges, *Philosophy of the Urban Guerrilla*, William Morrow, New York, 1973, p 233
3 The quotations from Marighela are taken from his '*For the Liberation of Brazil*', translated Butt & Sheed, Pelican, 1971
4 Evans, R. D., *Brazil: the Road Back from Terrorism*, Institute for the Study of Conflict, July, 1974

CHAPTER 13

The Future

'We're working for revolution all over the world'.

CARLOS MARTINEZ

Carlos Martinez, born Ilich Ramirez, in Caracas, Venezuela, in 1949, personifies the modern phenomenon of transnational terrorism. Dubbed 'the Jackal' by the world's Press, Carlos seized the headlines with his raid on the Vienna meeting of the Organization of Petroleum Exporting Countries. In the service of their ideology such men and women are prepared to help any movement which they see as attacking the capitalist system. Cosmopolitan in style and outlook, the international terrorists use modern communications systems to transport themselves, and the news of their exploits, to every corner of the world. Co-operation between terrorist movements makes tactical sense, even if their strategic objectives differ. Information on techniques of terror is exchanged. Expertise in bomb manufacture, weapon design, the uses of assassination and mass terror can be pooled. Governments, such as those of Uganda, Libya and Algeria, may from time to time ally themselves to terrorist movements and provide them with a base.

Terrorists like Carlos see themselves as actors on the international stage; in their own eyes they are as legimate as the governments, international organizations and multinational companies which also have roles to play. They are entitled, therefore, to use diplomacy, including that of force, just as Governments are. In what way, they will ask, do they differ from the KGB or the CIA in their operations?

Alternatively they may argue that in specific cases a people, such as the Palestinians, is just as entitled to armed forces and a secret service as are 'sovereign states', whose legitimacy rests ultimately only on a superiority of force within a defined geographical area. Indeed, they will suggest that while States have many ways of exerting their influence, groups such as the Palestinians, Basques or Bretons can only achieve a hearing through violence.

The attraction of violence to such people, whether in support of anarchists, separatists or Palestinians, is that it can be seen as simultaneously weakening the capitalist system and its arch-protector the 'imperialist' United States. Since sovereign States have their organizations of co-operation, such as NATO, it is 'logical and necessary' for terrorists to do likewise.

Carlos, born in Venezuela, educated in London and Moscow, was trained as a guerrilla in the Lebanon. The Latin America from which he came is full of terrorist groups which, with the failure of the largely Cuban-backed revolutions in the 1960s, now co-operate on a world-wide scale. The Chilean *Movement of the Revolutionary Left*, the *Army of National Liberation* in Bolivia and the Trotskyist *People's Revolutionary Army* of Argentina have linked with the rump of the Uruguayan *Tupamaros* (the *Movement of National Liberation*); their organization reportedly has offices in Lisbon, Paris and Rome. Carlos had contact with Cuban diplomats (three were subsequently expelled from France) during his stay in Paris. Castro still offers training facilities for guerrillas and the Soviet Union makes use of his relatively favourable image to use Cuba as her proxy in the Third World.[1] The Trotskyists continue to use their international network to support terrorism. The Argentinian *ERP* guerrillas broke with the Brussels-based Trotskyist *Fourth International* in 1973 but a splinter group (the 'Red Faction') remained affiliated. Money from kidnappings in Latin America has been passed to the *Fourth International*, which in turn has close connections with Palestinian terrorist

142

groups and whose German affiliate publicly supported the Baader-Meinhoff anarchist gang.[2] The Spanish section of the *Fourth International* has split, one group being opposed to terrorism as a tactic at the moment, while the other actively supports the Basque terrorist *ETA* organization.

The USSR is of course also fishing in these troubled waters; the main thrust of its effort after the Angolan success is now directed towards the training of guerrillas and saboteurs for southern Africa. The KGB presence in the area was sharply increased during 1976 and the number of Africans undergoing training in the USSR and Eastern Europe was then reported to be about 7,000.

The international web is yet more complicated. German anarchists of the Baader-Meinhoff group were trained in Palestinian camps in the Lebanon. The involvement of Gabriele Tiedemann and Hans Joachim Klein in operations directed by Carlos Martinez is not therefore surprising.

In September, 1970, Palestinian delegates visited North Korea; it is probable that contact was made at that time with members of the fanatical Japanese Red Army, whose members were still in Korea after hi-jacking a Japanese airliner the previous May. Two years later a Japanese Red Army group was responsible for the Lod airport massacre. In May, 1972, the *Popular Front for the Liberation of Palestine* held a co-ordinating meeting for the world's terrorists in the Lebanon; representatives from West Germany, Turkey, Iran and Ireland attended. The *Official IRA* has twice organized conferences for 'anti-imperialist' groups.

All these contacts occur in the shadowy and shifting world of transnational terrorism—they will be made and broken as expediency dictates but, at any time, there will exist a chain of communication and logistics which is available to any terrorist group seeking assistance, advice or finance.

To what extent can such activities be called 'revolutionary'? They constitute, of course, an arrogant élitism of the most obvious kind. Terrorists do not concern themselves with social conditions but, on the contrary, impose a random misery and death in order to persuade Governments to make concessions. They do not consult 'the people' but follow only their own ideological preferences.

Today the link between terrorism and economic and social change is exceedingly tenuous. The terrorists' argument would probably be that 'US Imperialism' is the great prop of 'repressive régimes' and that any act which weakens the United States contributes to 'world revolution'. Action against Zionism would be justified in the same way. In general by forcing 'bourgeois governments' to take stern measures to deal with violence, the terrorist may hope to shake public confidence and force a polarization of opinion between liberals and conservatives, both inside target countries and internationally.

Lenin argued that war was the great opportunity for revolution; today terrorism is the closest the revolutionary can get to it.

NOTES

1 See Colebrook, Joan, *New Lugano Review*, Vol 8–9, 1976
2 For an account of the complicated affairs of the *Fourth International*, see *Hearings Before the Internal Security Sub-committee*, 94th Congress, First Session, 24 July, 1975, US Government Printing Office, Washington, DC

INDEX

146

Organization of Latin American Solidarity, 130, 133
Organization of Petroleum Exporting Countries, 10, 120, 141

Pak Hon-yong, 95
Paris Commune, 28, 32n
Pfrimer, Dr Walter, 49
Pham Boi Chau, 86
Pham Van Dong, 80
Pike, Douglas, 94n
Plekhanov, 27
Poehner, Ernst, 50
Popular Front for the Liberation of Palestine, 143
Populorum Progressio, 122
Populists, 4, 24
Possony, Stefan T., 32n

Radek, 3
Rasputin, 21
Red Army (Japanese), 143
Rees, David, 100n
Reflections on Violence, 15, 17n
Revolutionary Communist Party of Brazil, 130, 133
Rex Party, 48
Rivera, Primo de, 49
Roehm, Captain, 52n

Sacco, 13
Von Sanders, Liman, 71, 75
Sand, Georges, 32n
Scalopino, R., 17n, 100n
Schram, S., 17n, 66n, 67n
Shakespeare, 17n
Shukman, 31n, 32n
Smith, Irving H., 43n
Socialist Revolutionaries, 25, 26, 36
Sorel, Georges, 2, 15, 16, 17n
SS, 48, 50, 52n
Stahlhelm, 47
Stalin, Stalinism, 23, 33, 34, 35, 53, 58, 60, 98, 99, 103

Stolypin, 39
Storrs, Sir Ronald, 69, 79n
Students for a Democratic Society, 17n
Sturmabteilungen (SA), 47, 48, 50
Suleiman Mousa, 77
Sun Tzu, 60–1
Svechin, 41
Szalasi, Ferenc, 48

Taratuta, Victor, 31
Thomas, Hugh, 109n
Thoughts of Chairman Mao, The, 14
Tiedemann, Gabriele, 143
Tito, 100n
Truong Chinh, 90–1
Ts'ao Ts'ao, 63
Tsunyi Conference, 53
Tukhachevsky, 41
TUPAMAROS, 2, 7, 122, 142

Ulyanov, Alexander, 19, 24
Union of the Russian People, 49
United Nations, 10
Ustashe, 111

Vallières, 13
Vanzetti, 13
Villars, J. B., 70, 74, 79n

Warner, Denis, 92
Washington, George, 85
Wavell, A. P., 77, 79n
White Negroes of America, 13
Wingate, Sir Reginald, 77
Wretched of the Earth, The, 17n

Yellow Shirts, 49

Zeid, Sheikh, 77
Zimmerwald Conferences, 21
Zionism, 37, 144

147